KIDS DRAW MANGA SHOUJO

CHRISTOPHER HART

WATSON-GUPTILL PUBLICATIONS
NEW YORK

To Isabella
and Francesca

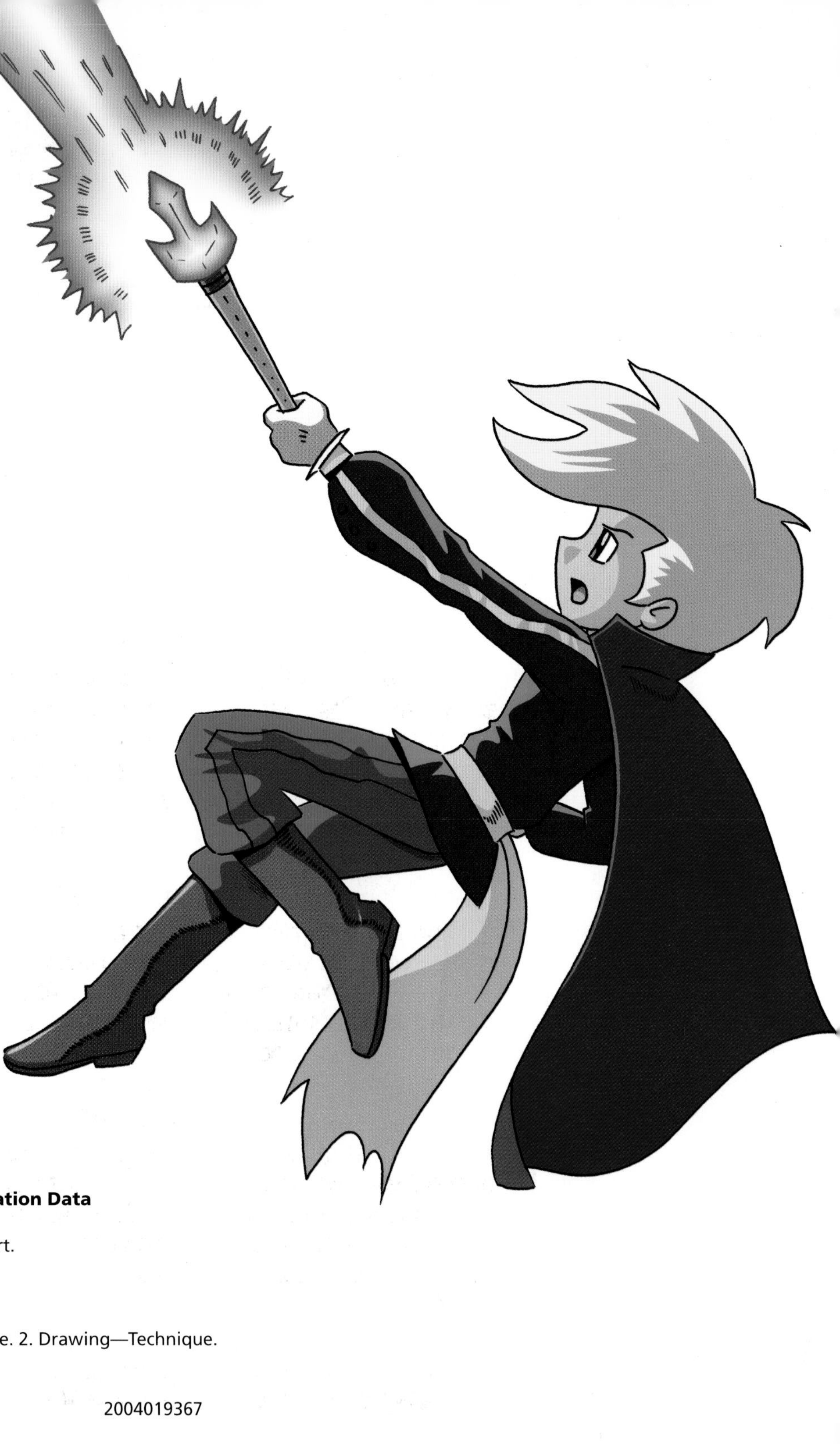

Senior Acquisitions Editor: Julie Mazur
Project Editor: Laaren Brown
Designer: Bob Fillie, Graphiti Design, Inc.
Production Manager: Hector Campbell
Text set in 12-pt. Frutiger Roman

First published in 2005 by
Watson-Guptill Publications,
a division of BPI Communications, Inc.,
770 Broadway, New York, NY 10003
www.watsonguptill.com

Library of Congress Cataloging-in-Publication Data
Hart, Christopher.
Kids draw Manga Shoujo / Christopher Hart.
p. cm. — (Kids draw)
Includes index.
ISBN 0-8230-2622-1
1. Comic books, strips, etc.—Japan—Technique. 2. Drawing—Technique.
I. Title.
NC1764.5.J3H369284 2005
741.5-dc22 2004019367

Printed in China

First printing, 2005

2 3 4 5 6 7 8 / 12 11 10 09 08 07 06

CONTENTS

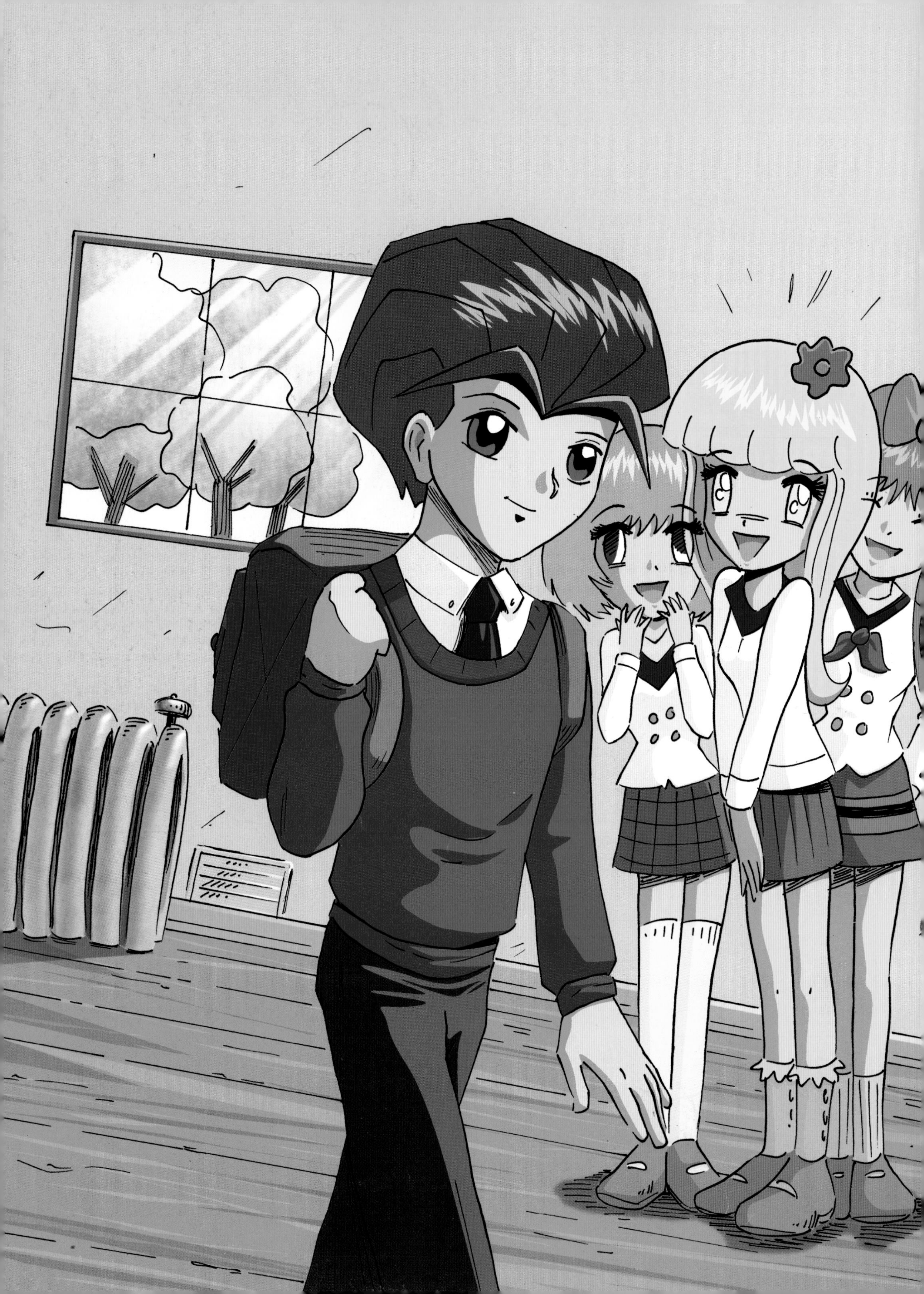

INTRODUCTION

Welcome to the wonderful world of manga shoujo! Shoujo is perhaps the best-loved style of Japanese comics, or "manga." It is based on the "big eye" characters that appeal equally to boys and girls.

While there is still plenty of adventure in shoujo, a lot of the stories center on friendship, loyalty, and teamwork. There are pretty girls and princesses, leading men and fantasy fighters, knights, fairies, fashionable teens, school kids, goddesses and demigods, and the popular "magical girls." Almost anything you can imagine can be part of manga shoujo.

This book makes drawing shoujo easy and fun. It's easy, because all of the drawings are broken down into crystal-clear steps that are simple to follow. You'll start by learning the basics, then quickly move on to creating classic characters with your own special touches.

It's fun, because the drawings look really cool—but they're simple to do. So pick up a pencil and get started. Impress your friends and make tons of great drawings with *Kids Draw Manga Shoujo!*

LET'S DRAW!

Ready to get started? Get your pencil and paper, and let's draw the basic shoujo-style head. Soon you'll be creating your own great shoujo characters!

Drawing Faces

Here's a typical, cheerful shoujo girl in a front view. See the crisscrossed lines on the first drawing? These guidelines will help you place the features on the face. The guidelines also let you make the eyes even with each other.

FRONT VIEW

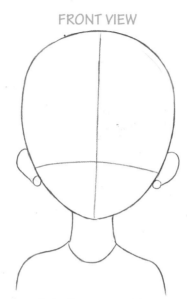

Draw light lines to guide you, then erase them at the end.

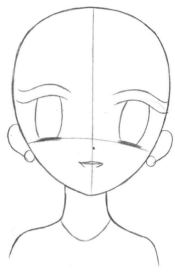

The nose starts as just a tiny dot. The top and bottom of the eyes are cut off by the eyelids.

Start penciling in details at this stage. Thick eyebrows and long bangs add to the shoujo look.

Details on the eyes add sparkle!

SIDE VIEW

Now we'll draw a boy in a side view, which is also called a "profile." The key to getting a good profile is drawing the nose in a sweeping curve. Shoujo boys also have receding chins—that is, they slope in rather than jutting out. Like girls' eyes, boys' eyes take up a lot of room on the face. The upper line of the eye is dark, and the bottom line is not. Look how the hair and eyes show this boy's personality!

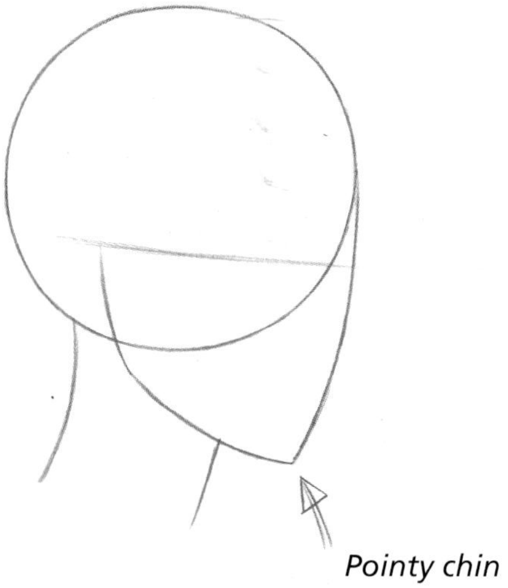
Pointy chin

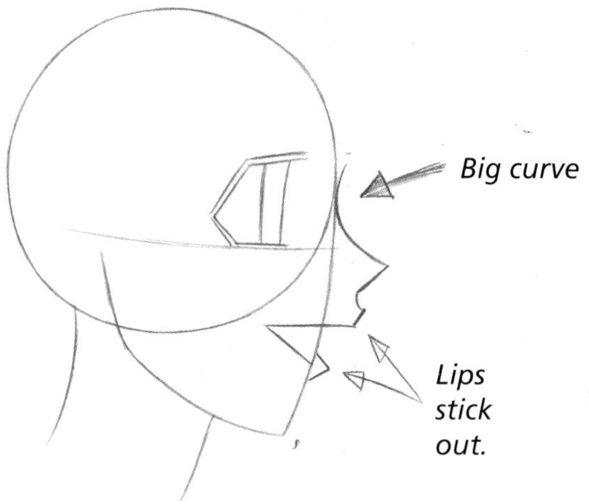
Big curve
Lips stick out.

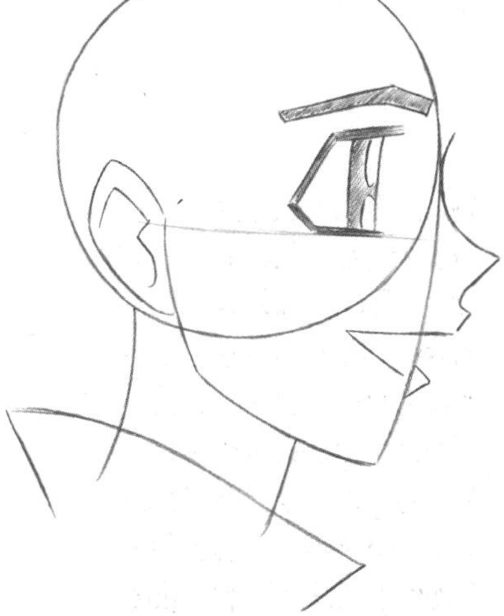

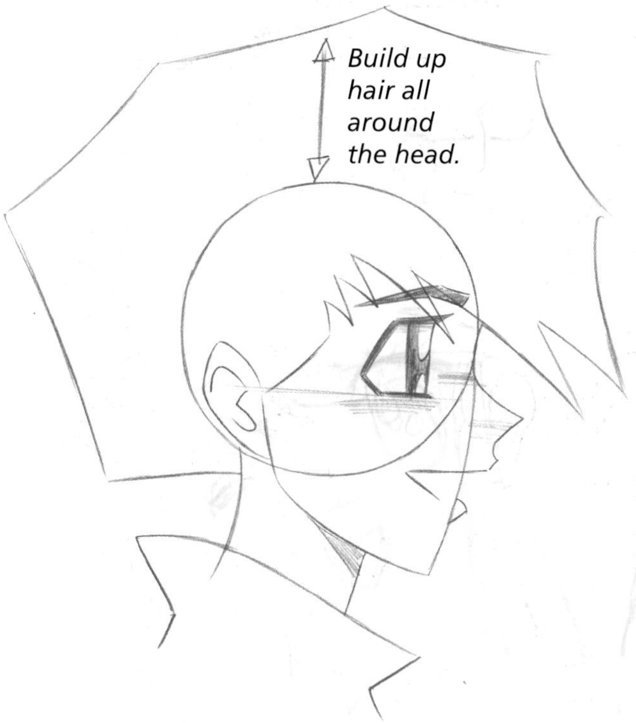
Build up hair all around the head.

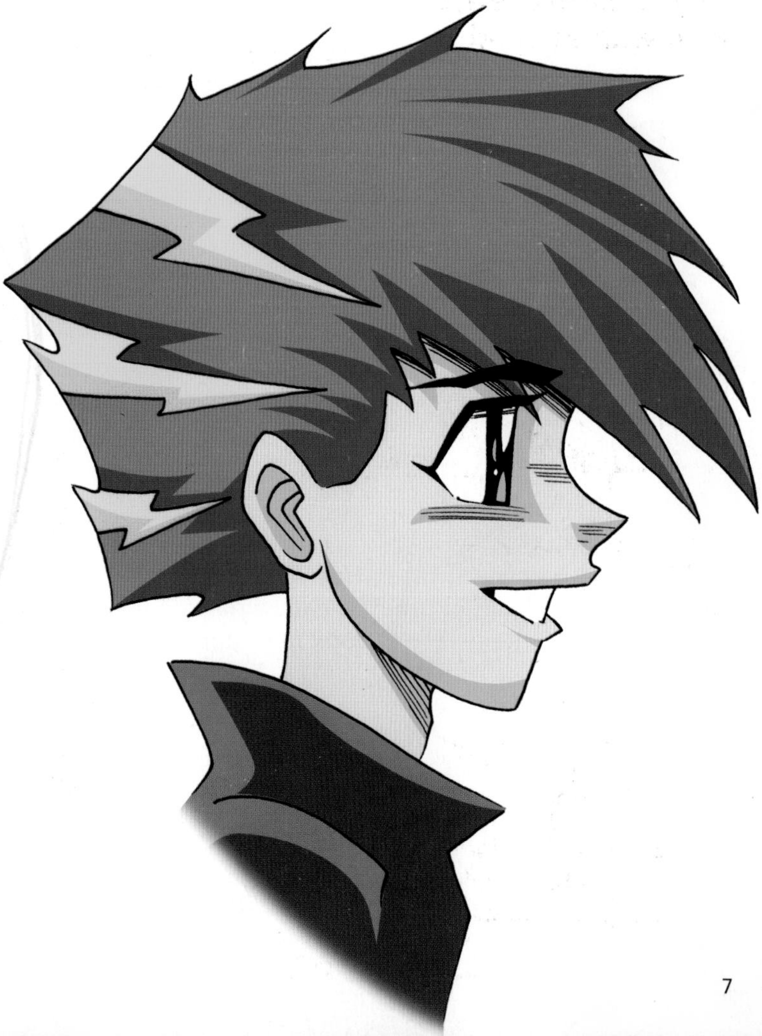

THREE-QUARTER VIEW

The three-quarter view is halfway between the front and side views. It's a popular pose, and it's my favorite, because it makes characters seem more lifelike. To make it simple, I've broken the process down into easy-to-follow steps, so that you can draw along with me.

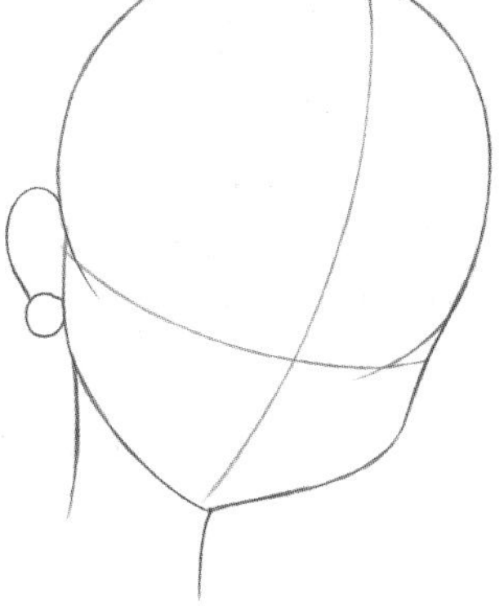

The center guideline is curved in this pose, never straight.

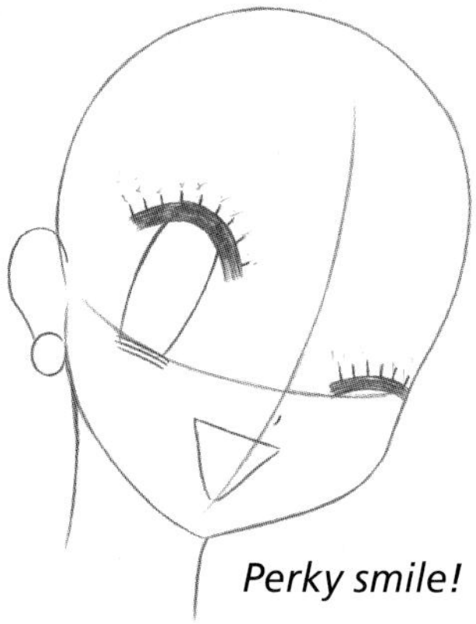

Perky smile!

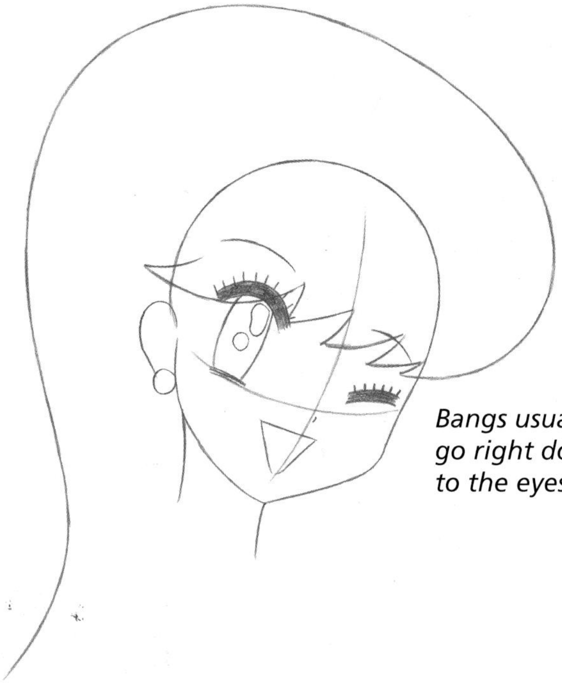

Bangs usually go right down to the eyes.

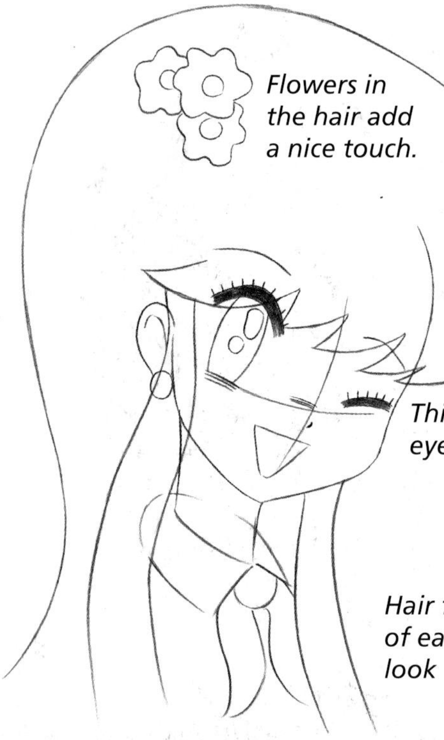

Flowers in the hair add a nice touch.

Thick eyelids

Hair falls in front of ears, a classic look in shoujo.

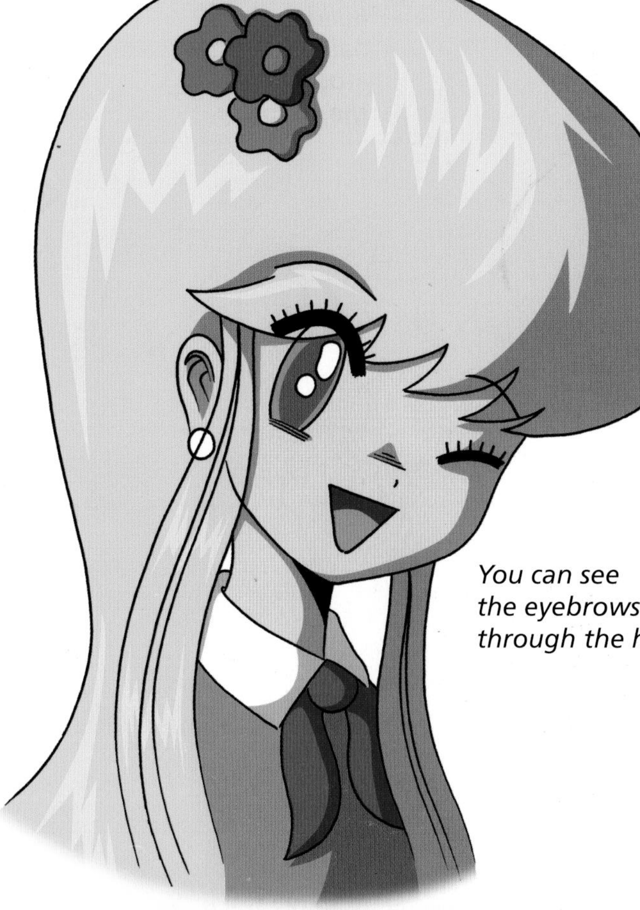

You can see the eyebrows through the hair.

Now let's look at a boy in a similar pose.

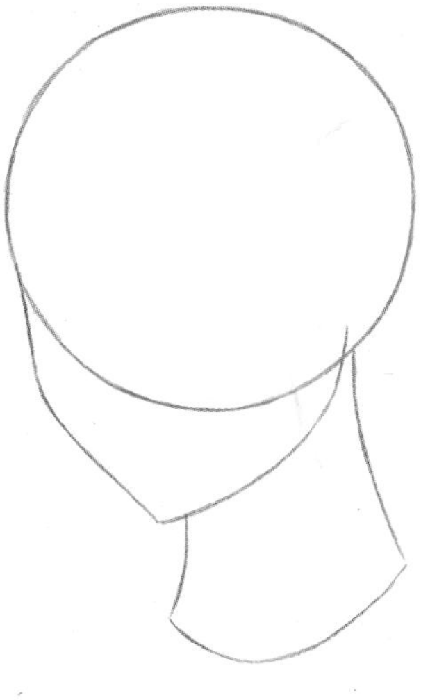

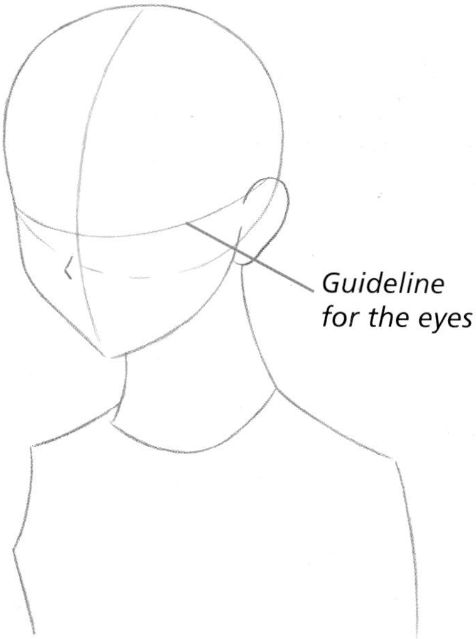

Guideline for the eyes

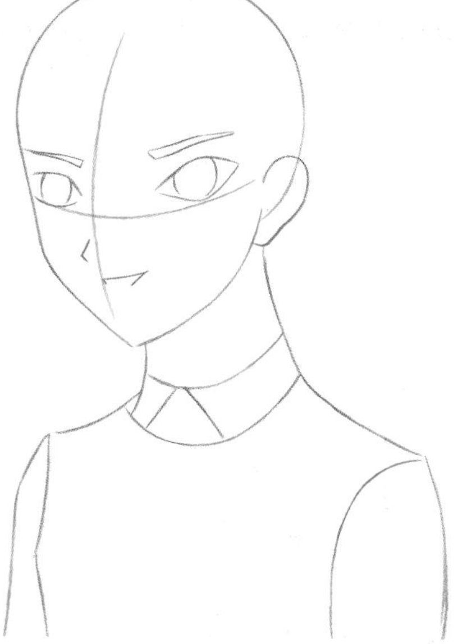

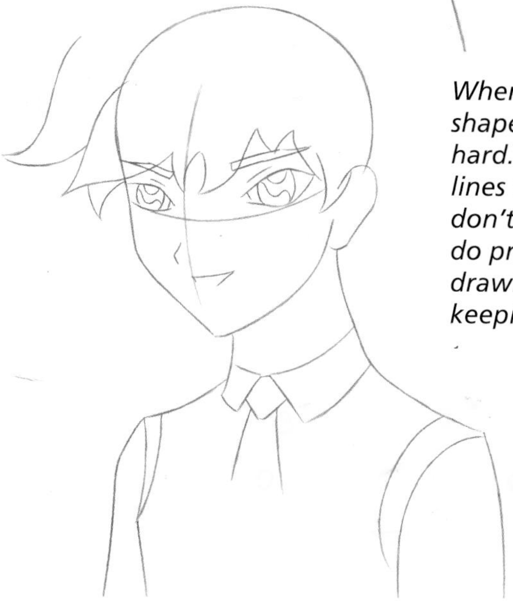

When you're sketching the basic shape of the head, don't press too hard. You'll want to erase the extra lines when you're finished and don't want them too dark. If you do press hard, just trace your drawing on a new sheet of paper, keeping only the lines you want.

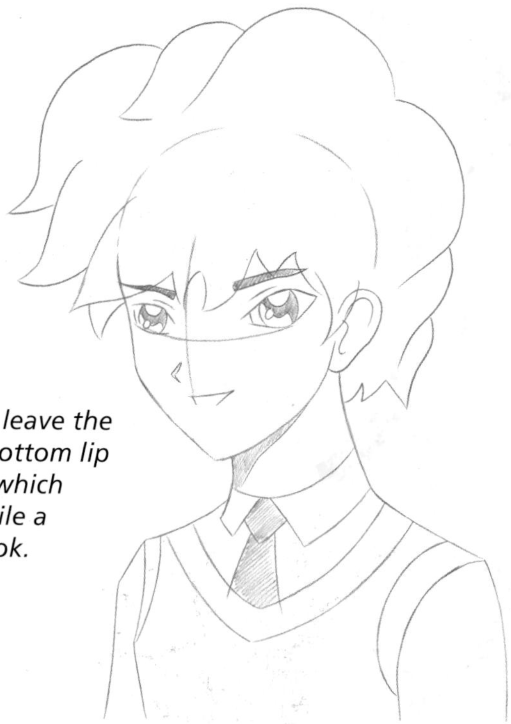

Sometimes I leave the line of the bottom lip unfinished, which gives the smile a gleaming look.

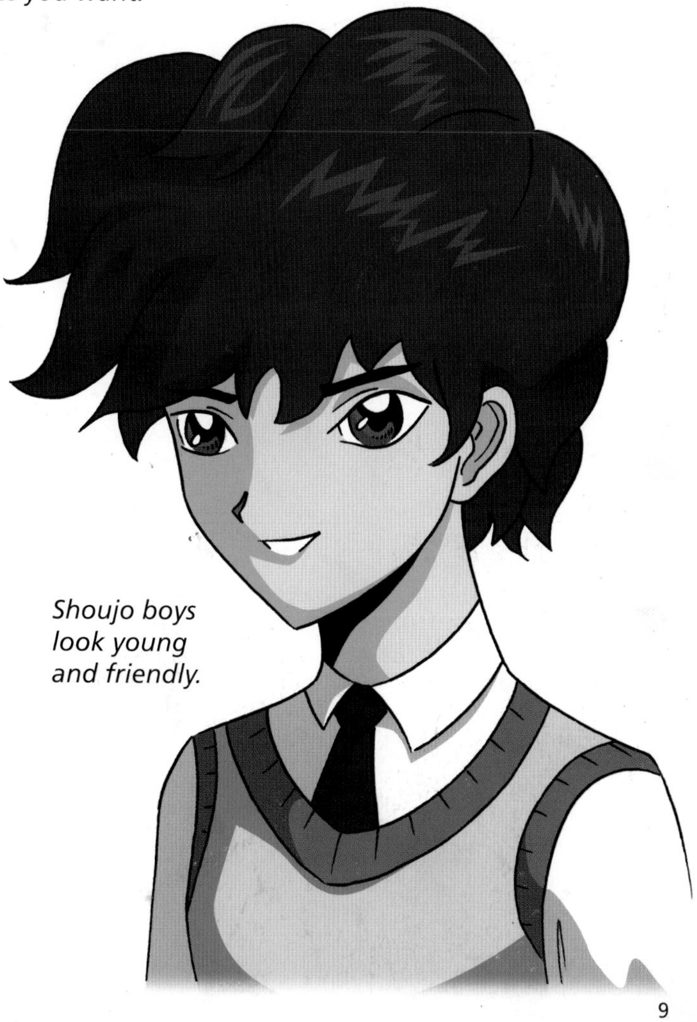

Shoujo boys look young and friendly.

Creating Girl Characters

Most female shoujo have certain traits in common. Use this page as a checklist when drawing your own characters. Bows, hair in a bun, flowers, or tiaras are frequently used to add a touch of femininity. Note the strands of hair that fall in front of the ears—they are typical in shoujo.

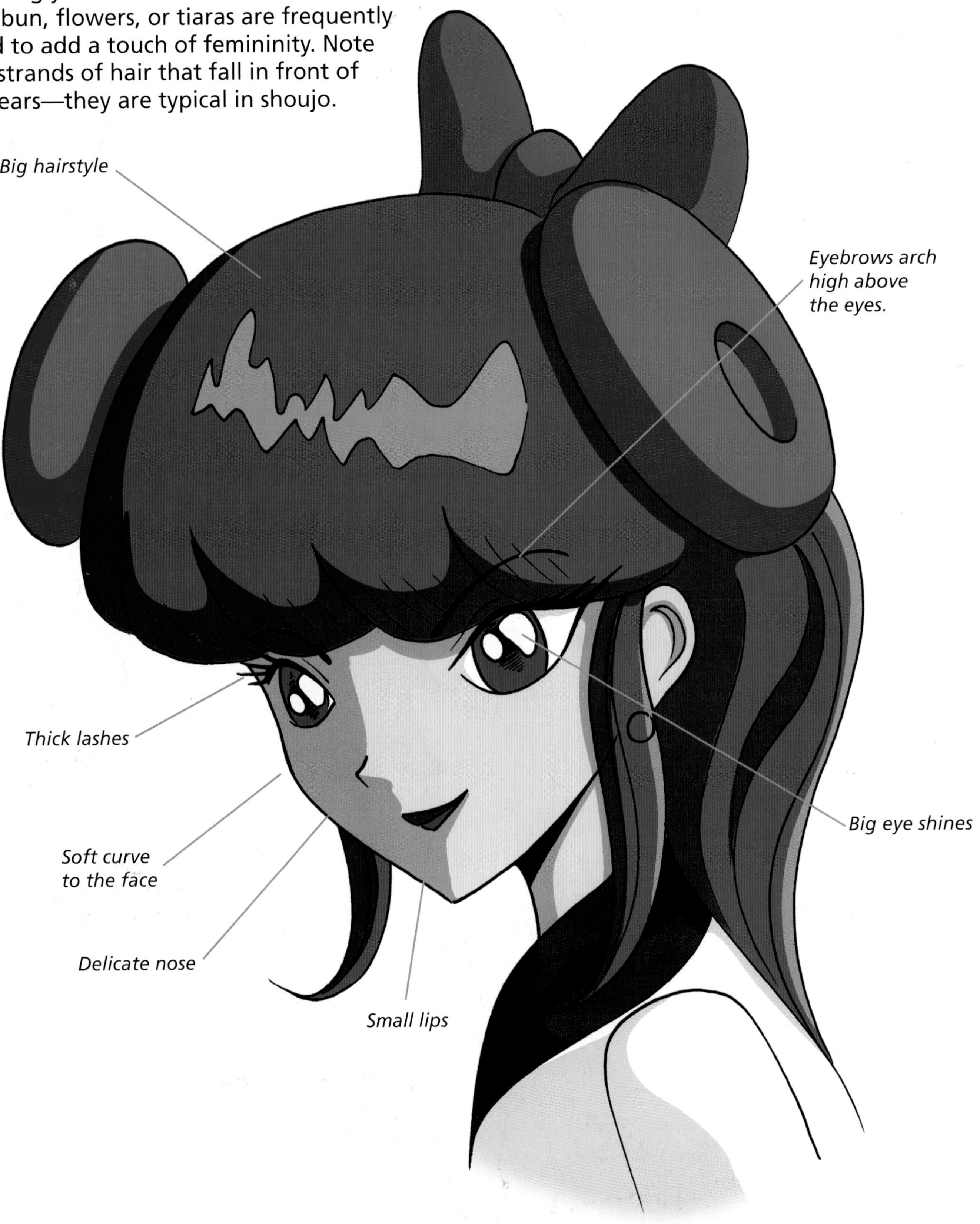

Big hairstyle
Eyebrows arch high above the eyes.
Thick lashes
Big eye shines
Soft curve to the face
Delicate nose
Small lips

Creating Boy Characters

Shoujo boys have an open, eager look. How do you show that personality in a drawing? Give your boy characters square jawlines and bright eyes. This boy is a good example: His eyebrows are thick and straight without eyelashes. Wild hair, styled or maybe a little messy, looks great!

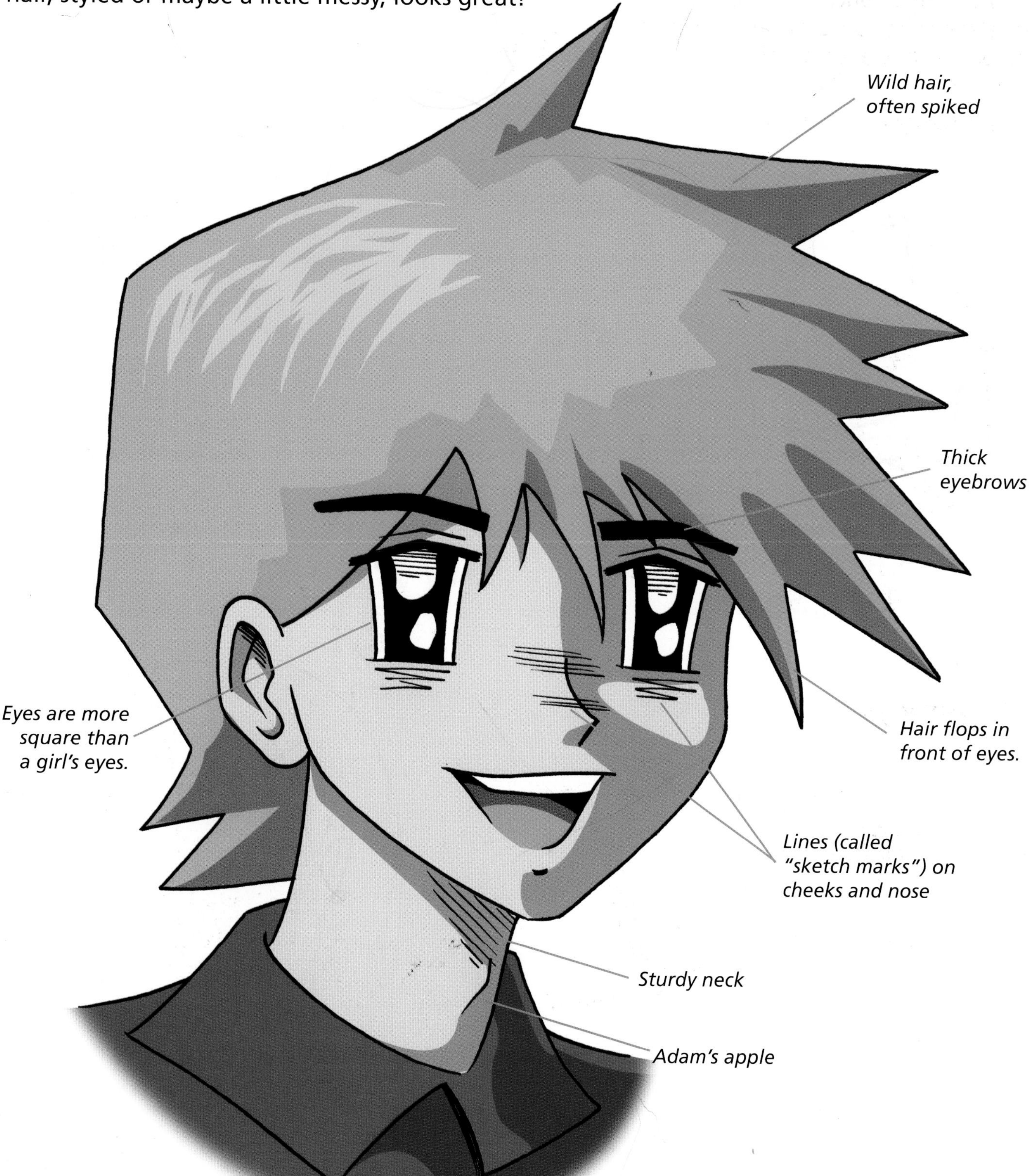

Wild hair, often spiked
Thick eyebrows
Eyes are more square than a girl's eyes.
Hair flops in front of eyes.
Lines (called "sketch marks") on cheeks and nose
Sturdy neck
Adam's apple

Drawing Bishies

The leading men of shoujo are dashing characters! In Japan, they are called Bishies, short for *bishonen,* which means "handsome man." While boys and girls have rounded faces, Bishies have long, thin faces. Their features are delicate: narrow eyes, sharp eyebrows placed right on top of the eyes, and long noses. Often, they have long hair parted down the middle.

FRONT VIEW

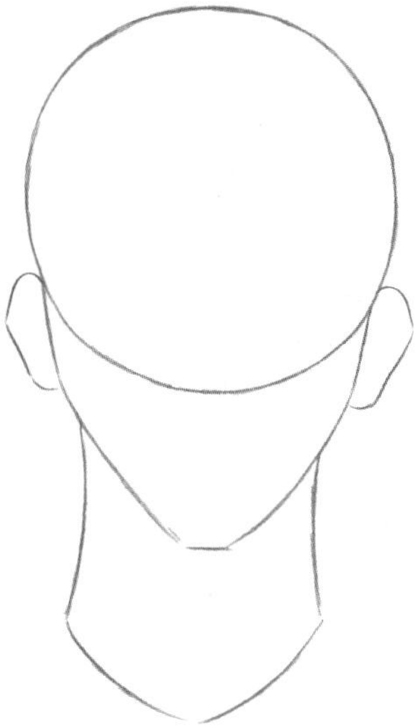

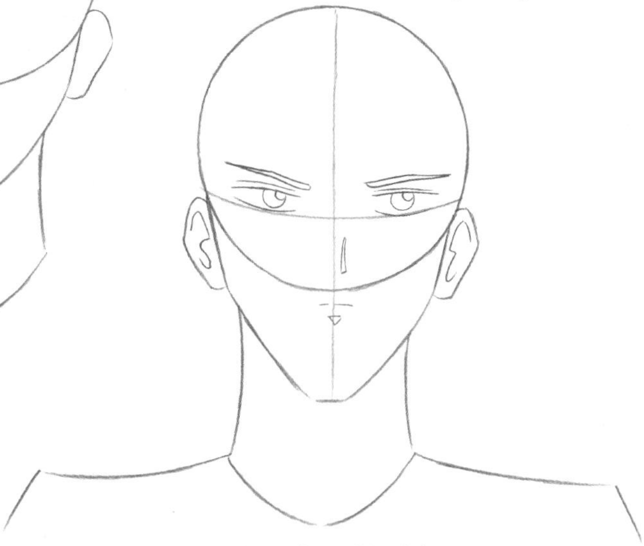

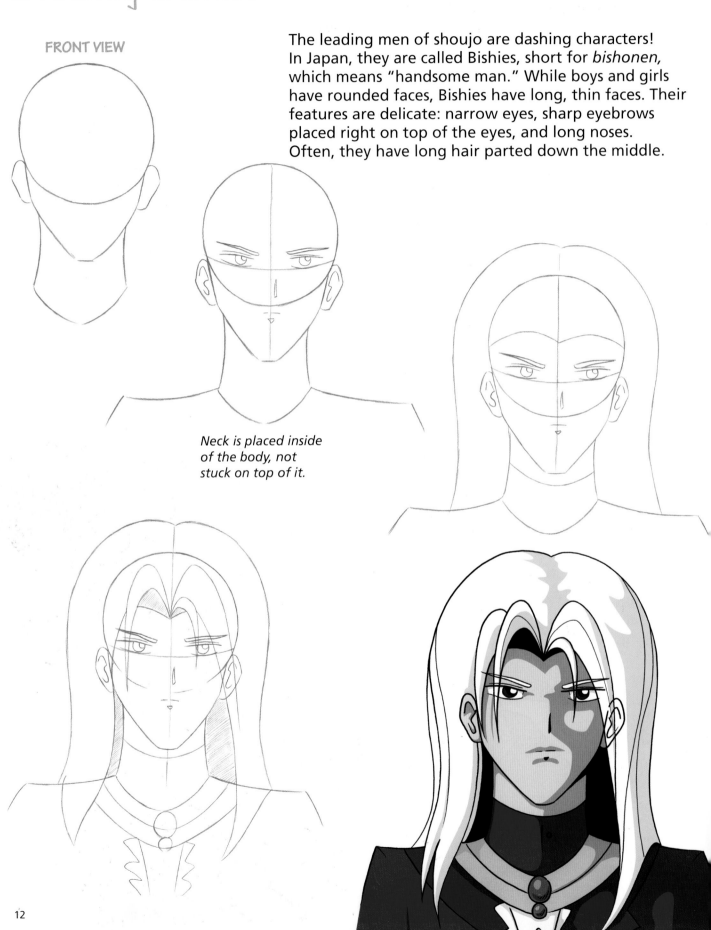

Neck is placed inside of the body, not stuck on top of it.

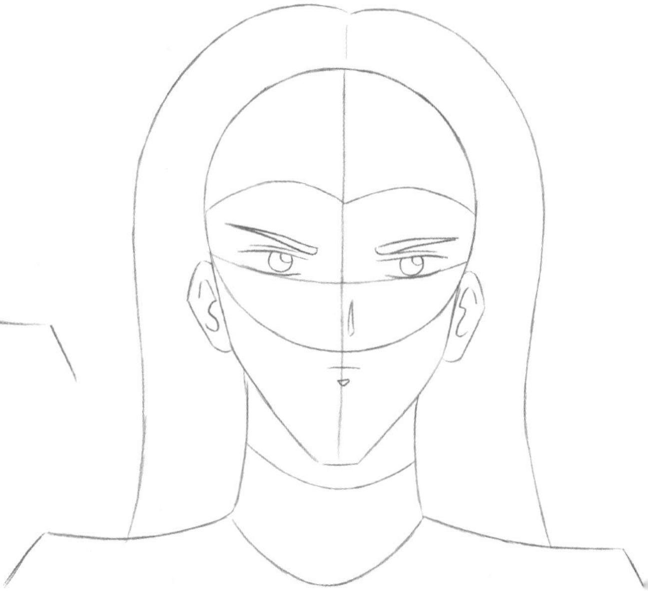

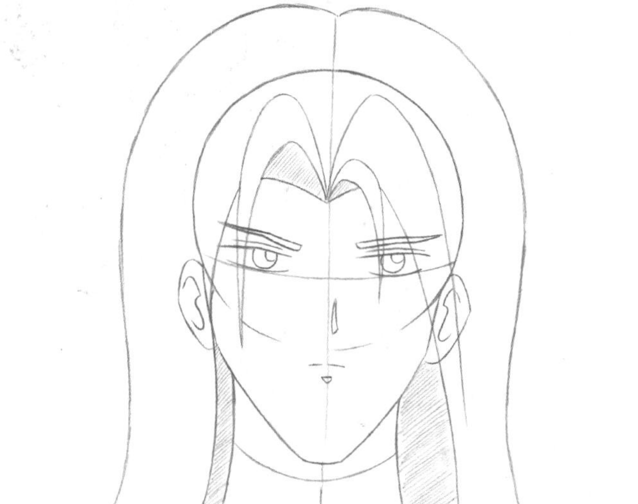

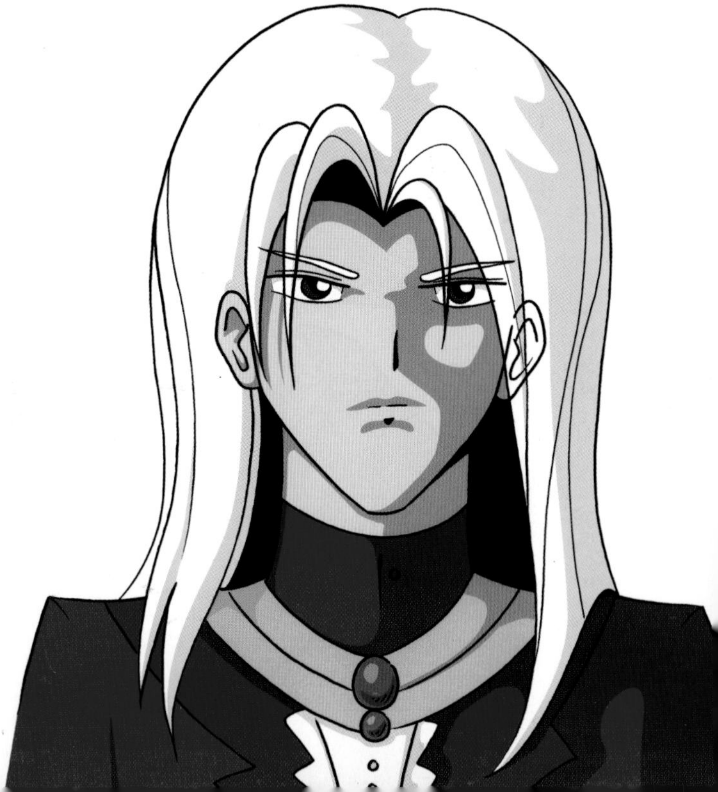

SIDE VIEW

When you look at a side view, you can see that the nose is very long on this type of character. Notice, too, that the neck does not attach to the base of the ear, but behind it. And yes, the neck really is that thick!

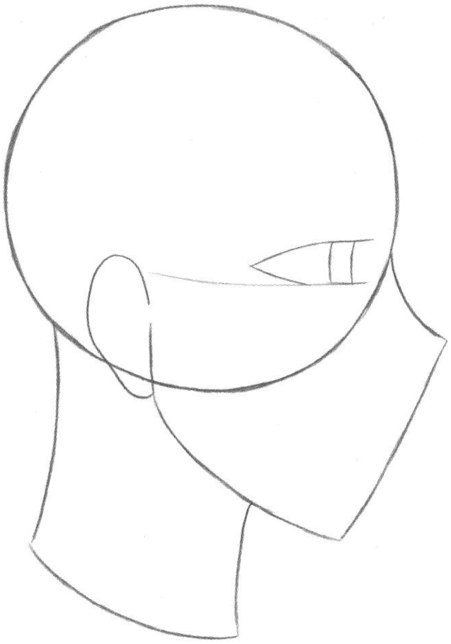

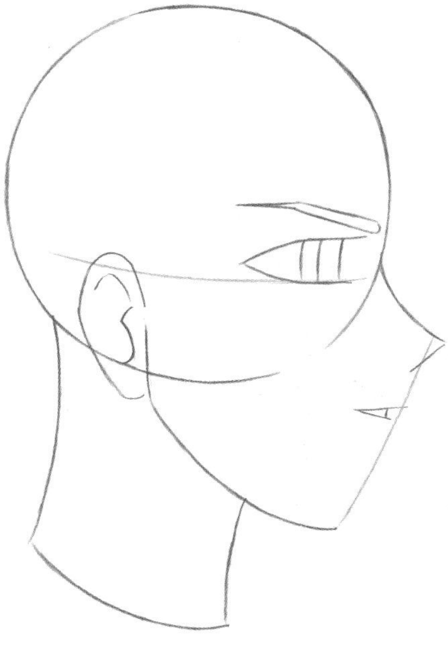

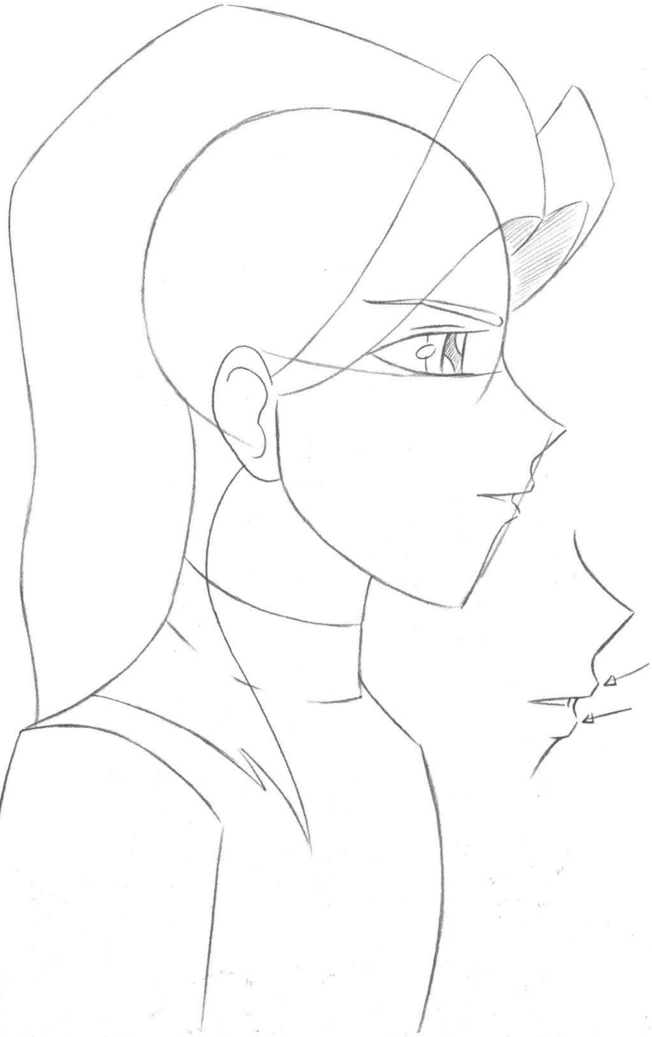

The lips stick out from the face.

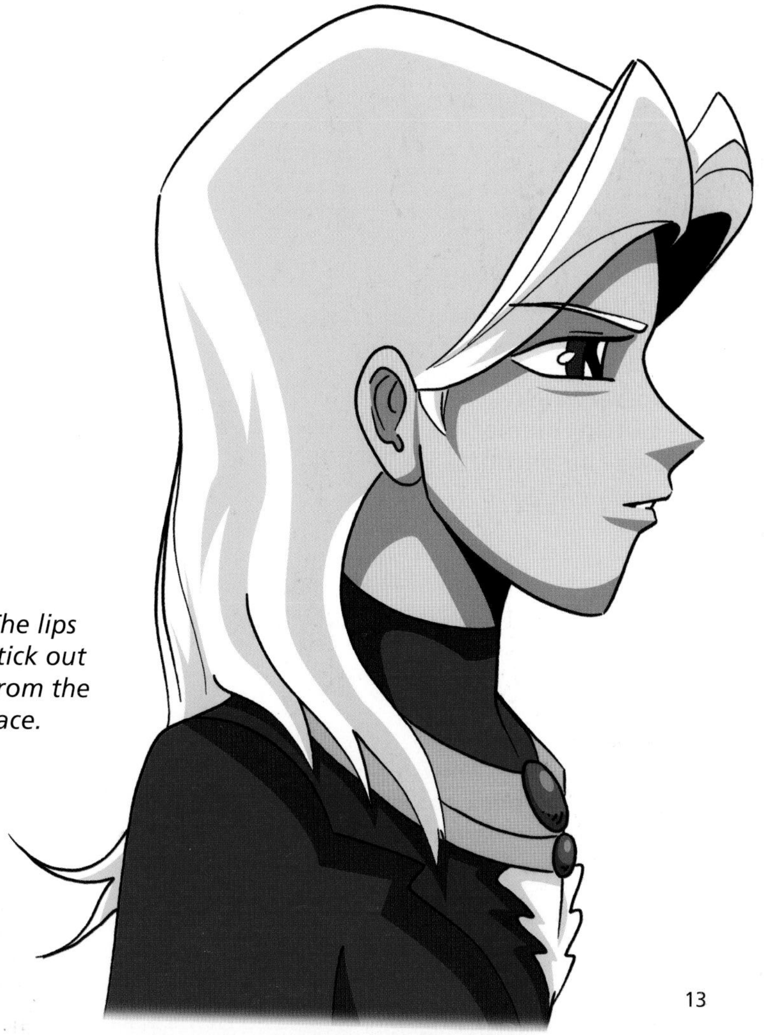

Creating Bishie Characters

Make your leading men unique by including these Bishie traits.

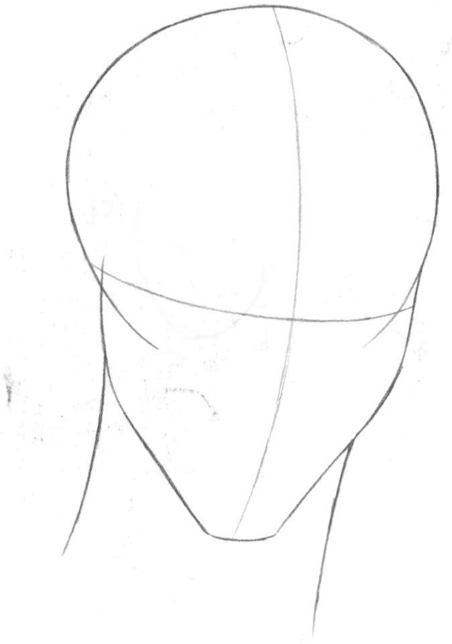

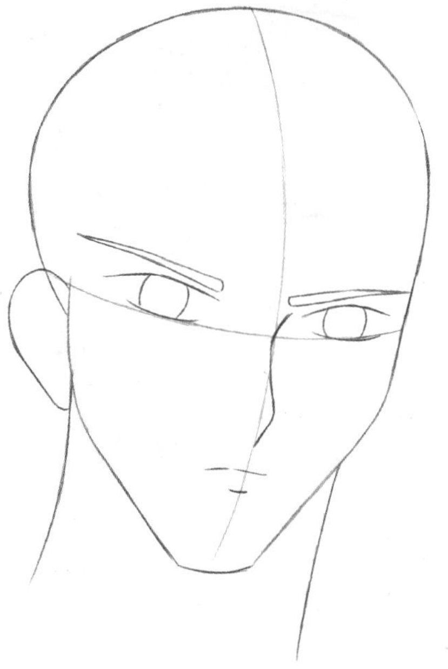

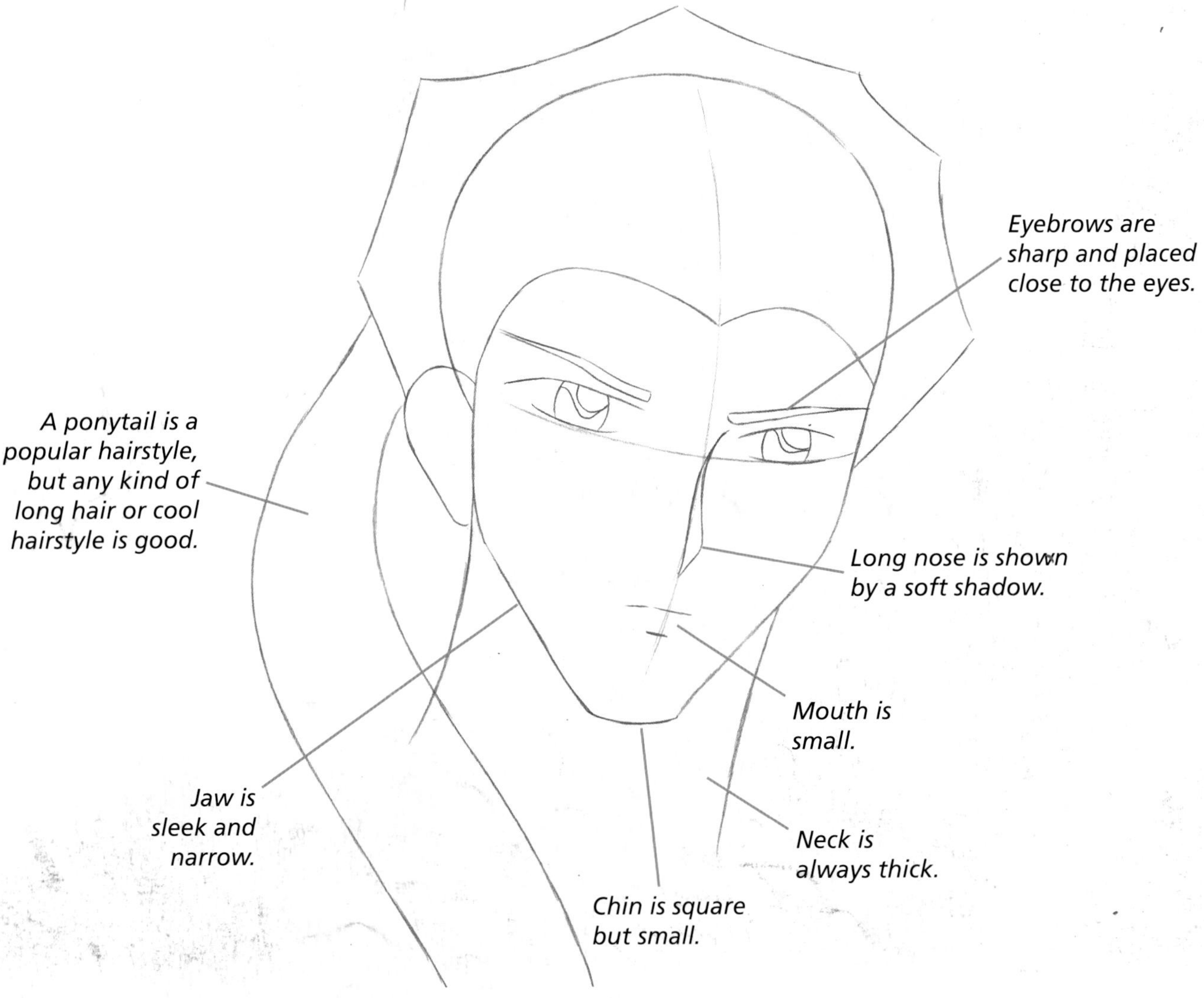
Eyebrows are sharp and placed close to the eyes.
A ponytail is a popular hairstyle, but any kind of long hair or cool hairstyle is good.
Long nose is shown by a soft shadow.
Mouth is small.
Jaw is sleek and narrow.
Neck is always thick.
Chin is square but small.

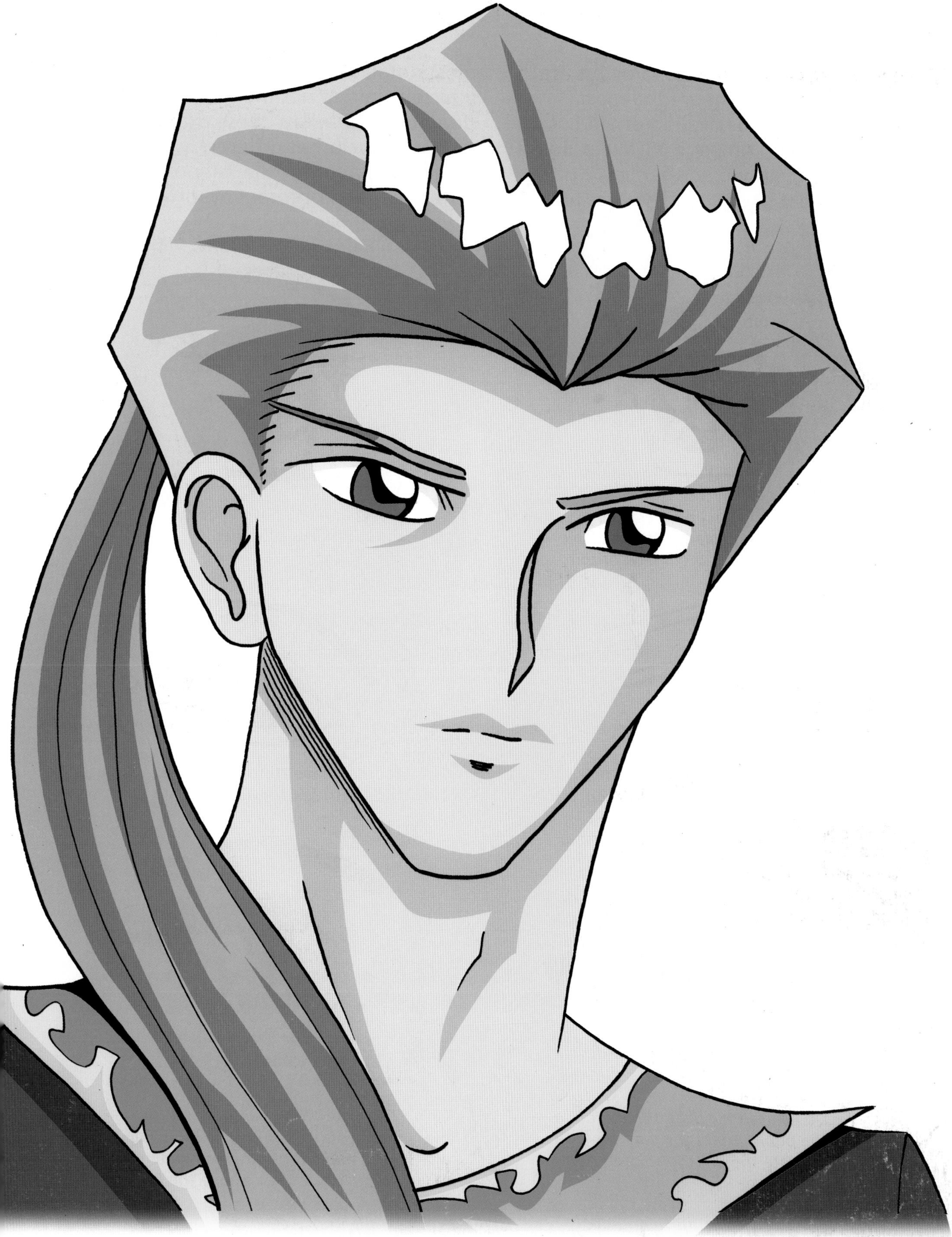

Drawing Eyes

The eyes of Japanese comic characters are famous, and shoujo eyes are the most brilliant, intense, and dazzling of all! Look at the leading man on page 15. What do his eyes tell you? What would they say if they were open wider or slitted? The eyes are the most detailed part of the face, so give yourself time to get them just right. You don't have to follow these examples exactly—draw the eyelashes differently, or create different shapes for the "shines" in the eyes or maybe even different eyebrows.

MALE EYES, FRONT VIEW

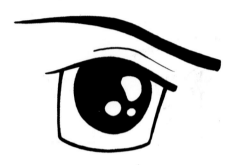

For young men and boys, the eyes are large and black, with multiple shines to make them look bright.

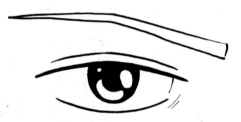

For men, including Bishies, the eyes have smaller eyeballs and a thinner shape.

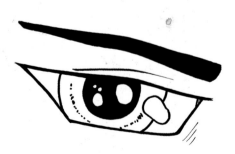

Do you see the dots going around the pupil? That's the way we indicate the iris, the colored part of the eye.

FEMALE EYES, FRONT VIEW

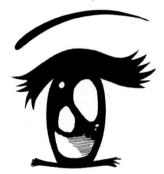

Girl characters have wide-open eyes with lots of shines.

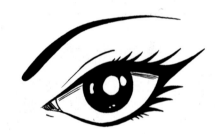

Women have almond-shaped eyes with feathery lashes.

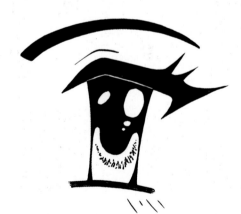

This type of eye can be used for both young girls and women. For girls, make it bright; for women, add the extra line above the lashes.

EYES, SIDE VIEW

In the side view, the basic shape of the eyes is the same for men and women. It changes for young and old characters, though.

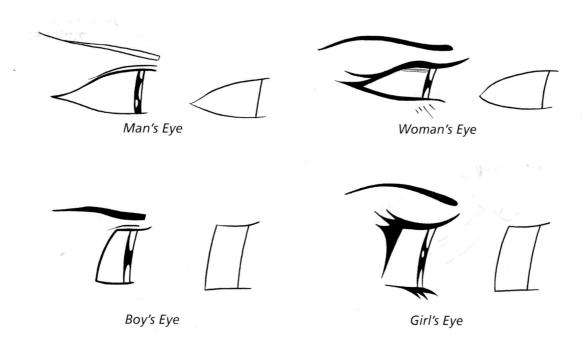

Man's Eye

Woman's Eye

Boy's Eye

Girl's Eye

Eyes, more than any other feature, show a shoujo character's personality. This girl is fun-loving yet thoughtful.

Here is the same girl in a side view. She has typical young female eyes—how would she look with different eyes? Try it!

Drawing the Female Body

Let your characters stand on their own two legs! Look how the female body is made up of basic shapes put together. Costumes cover these shapes, but your characters will look better if you understand the forms of each type of character—female, male, and Bishie.

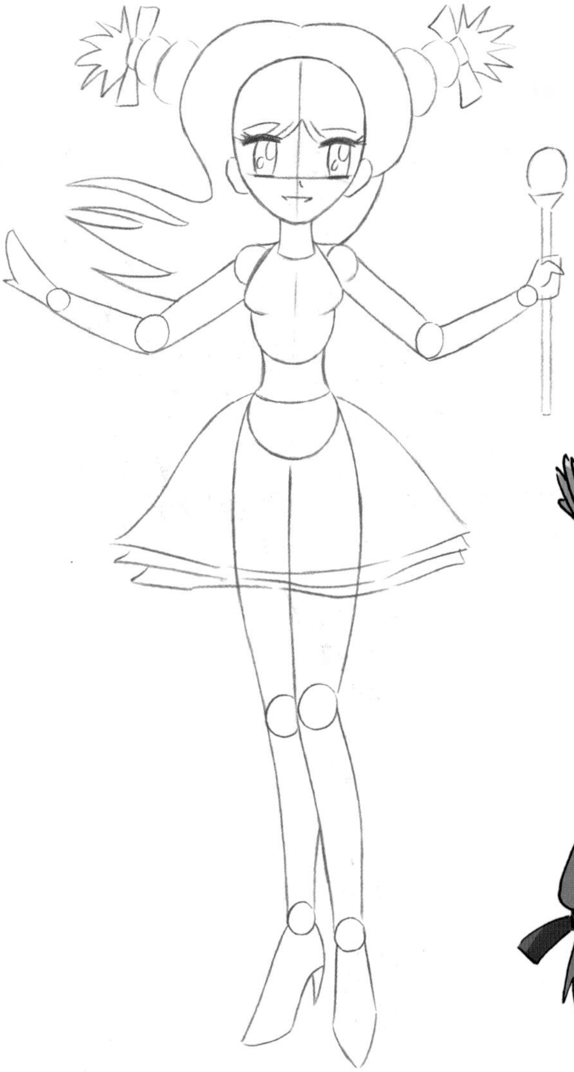

FRONT VIEW
Most magical girls have long legs and a narrow body.

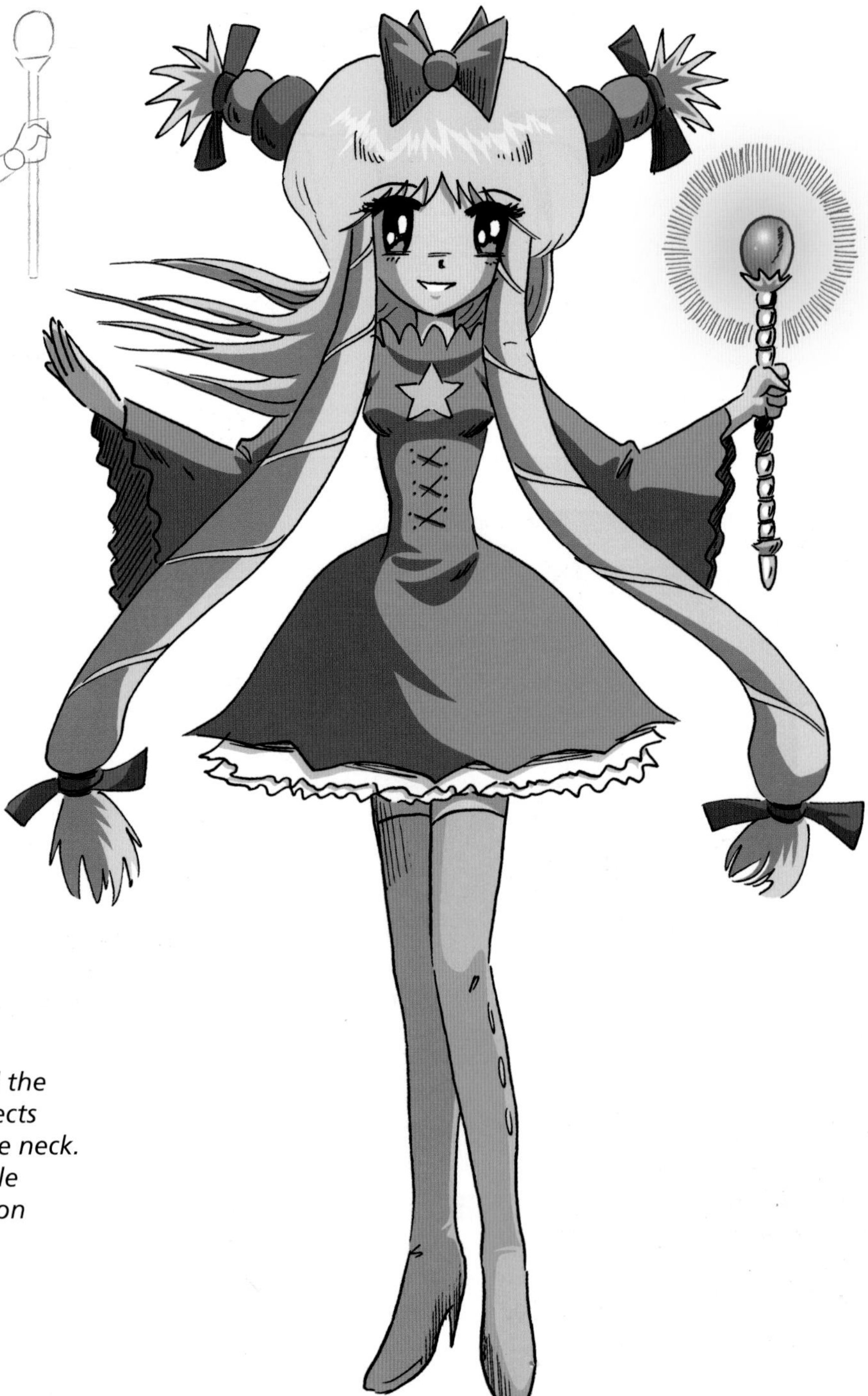

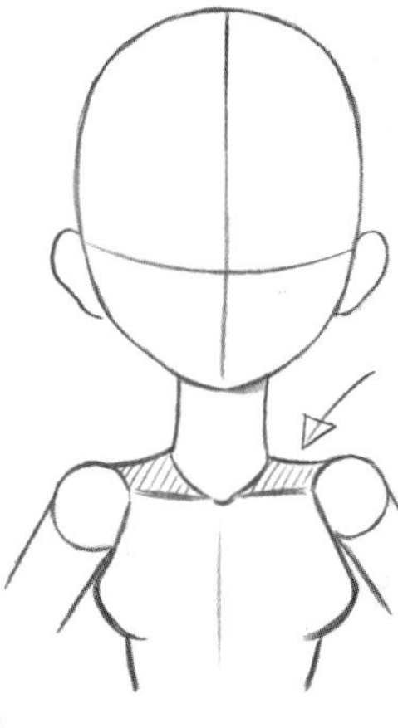

This muscle, called the "trapezius," connects the shoulder to the neck. It is small on female characters, larger on men and boys.

SIDE VIEW

Don't forget to draw both legs, even in the side view! You might be tempted to leave out the far leg, since it's hidden behind the front one. But that will look weird, as if one of her legs has disappeared. Instead, draw a hint of the far leg.

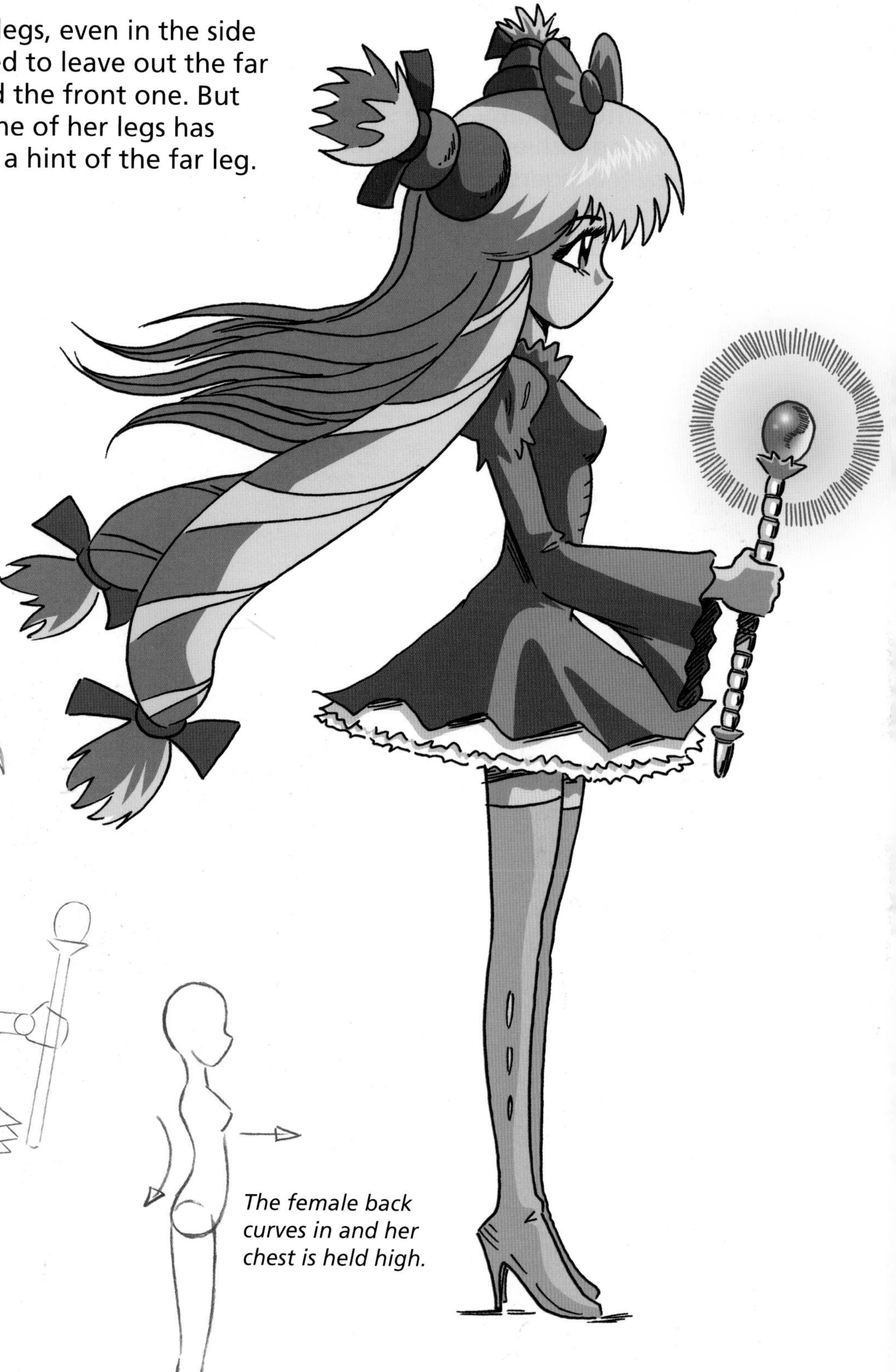

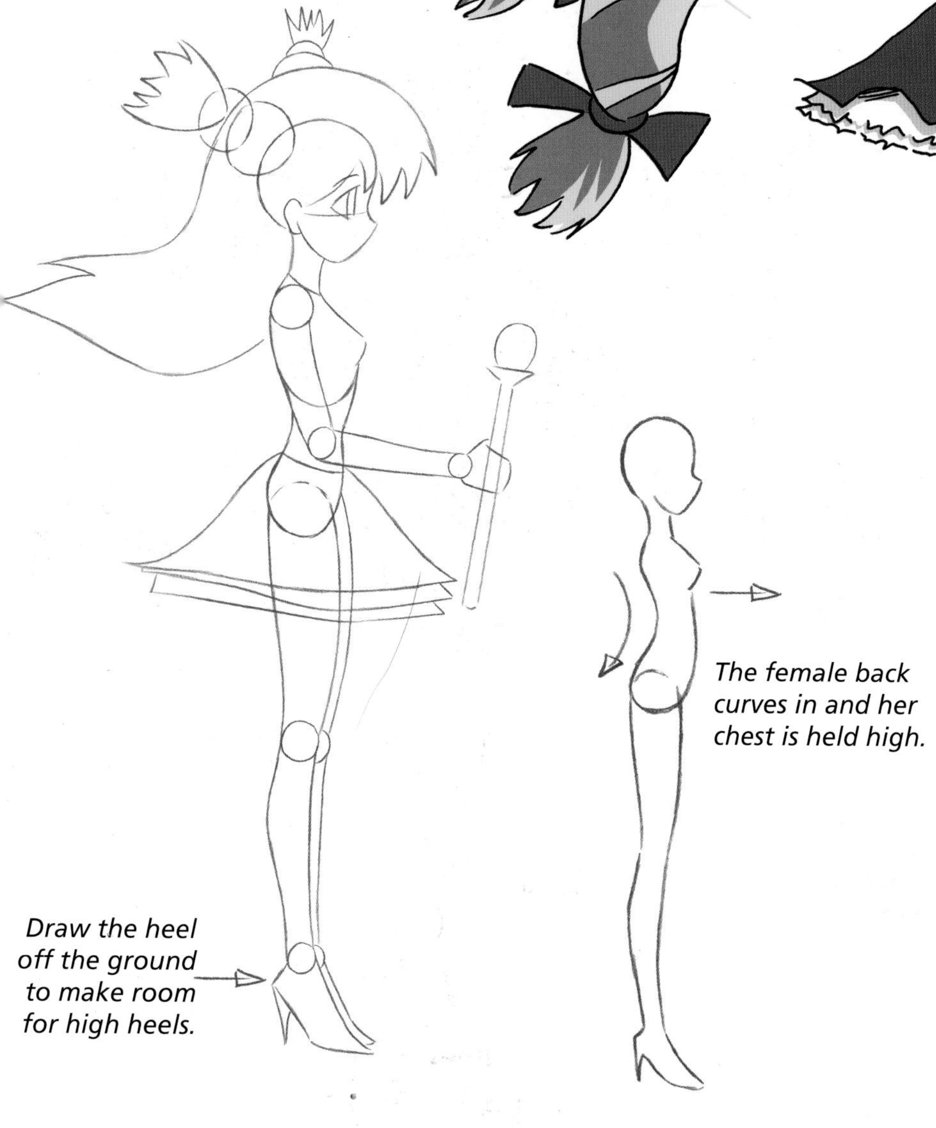
The female back curves in and her chest is held high.
Draw the heel off the ground to make room for high heels.

Drawing the Male Body

There are two different basic male shapes in shoujo: boys and Bishies. First let's look at how to draw teenagers or boys.

FRONT VIEW

Boys' chests are not much wider than their waists. Their arms can look a little muscular.

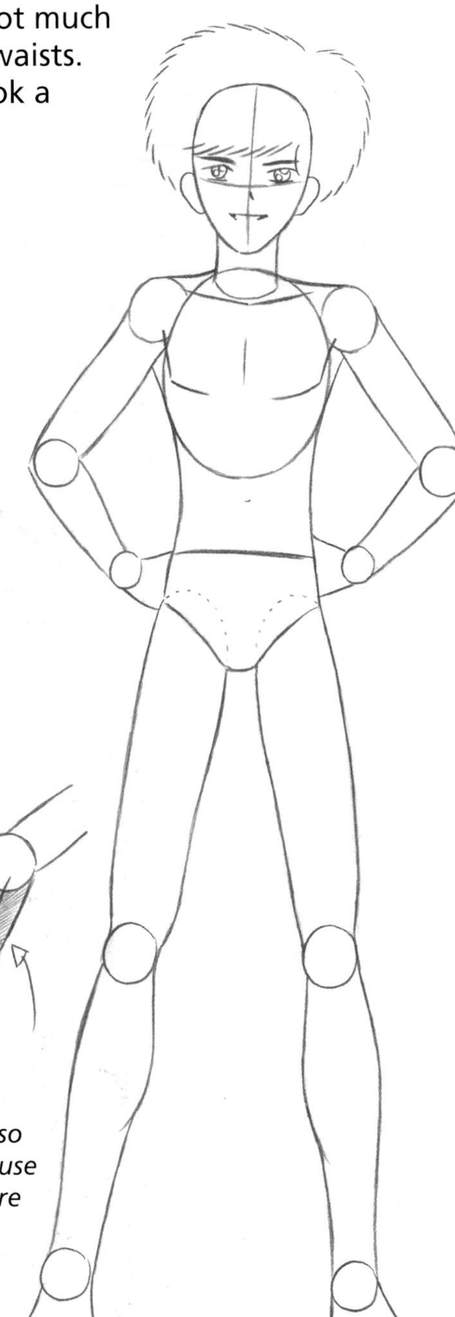

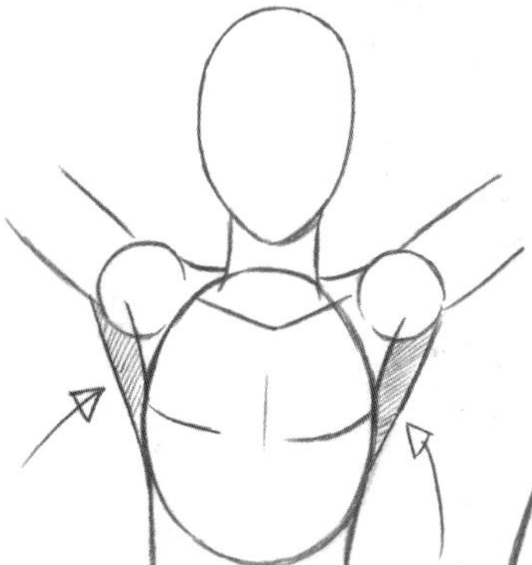

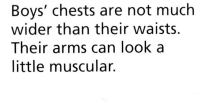

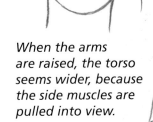

When the arms are raised, the torso seems wider, because the side muscles are pulled into view.

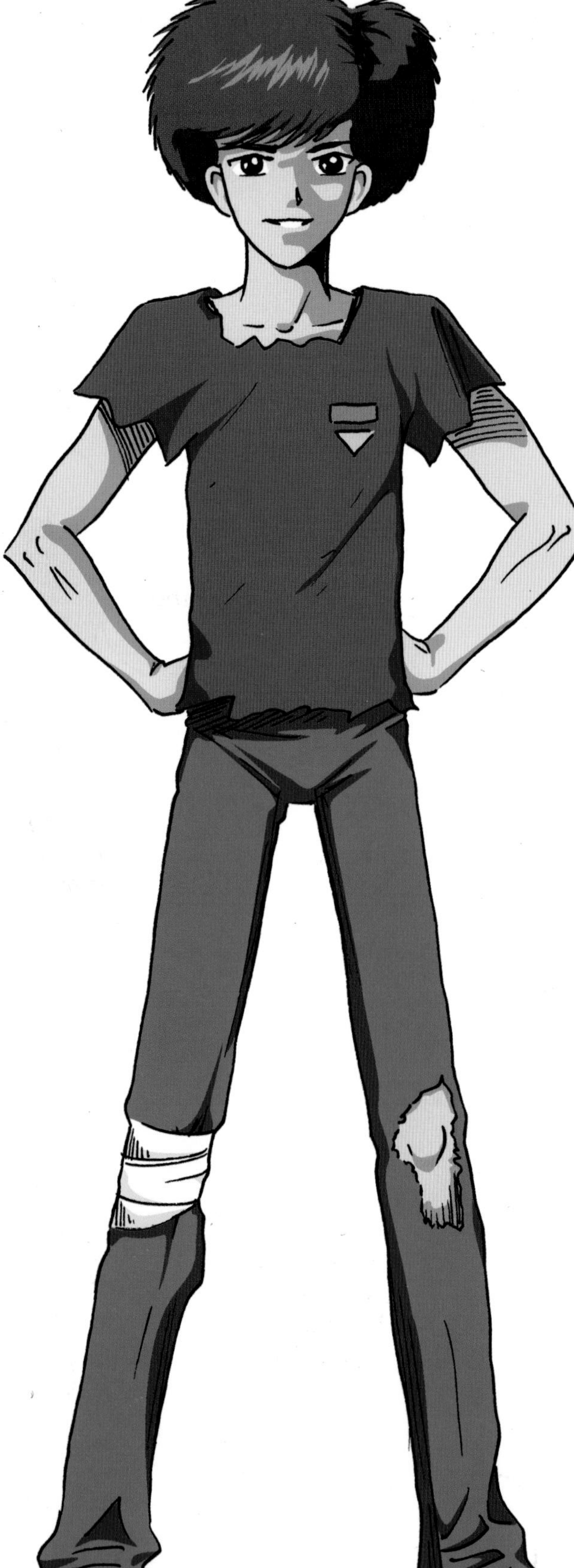

SIDE VIEW

In the side view, let the arms bend a bit at the elbow. If the arms are straight, the pose will look stiff and awkward.

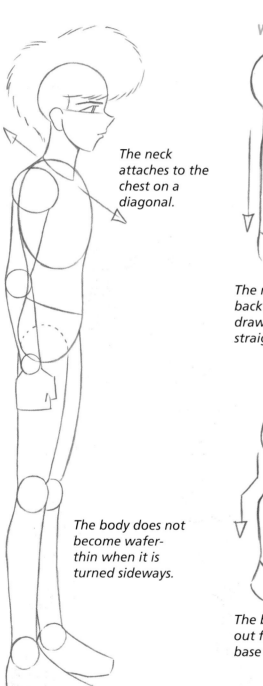

The neck attaches to the chest on a diagonal.

The body does not become wafer-thin when it is turned sideways.

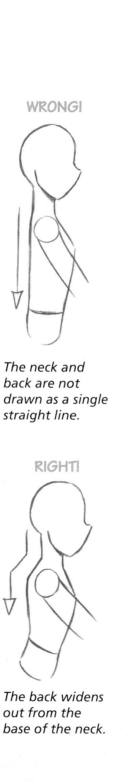

The neck and back are not drawn as a single straight line.

The back widens out from the base of the neck.

Drawing the Bishie Body

Bishies are smooth. They can be regal and wealthy or cool and trendy. They are also cast as fantasy characters, such as knights. Many shoujo stories have a Bishie.

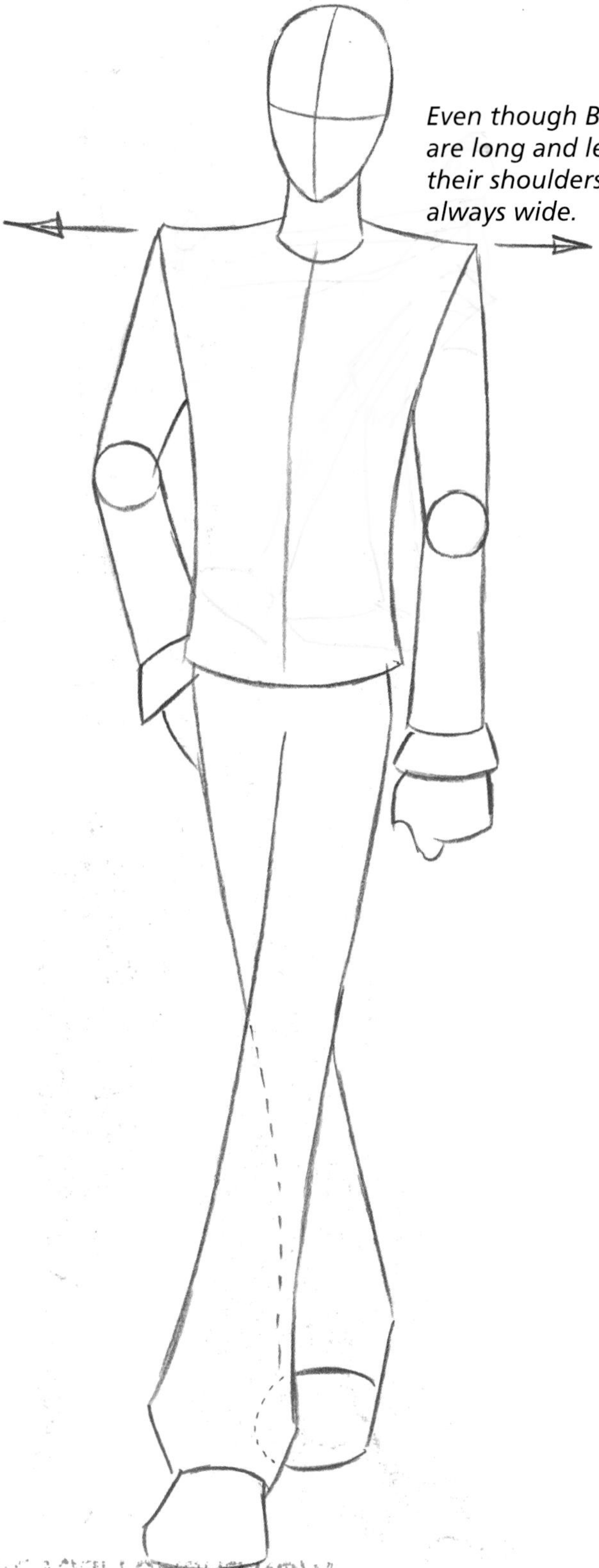

Even though Bishies are long and lean, their shoulders are always wide.

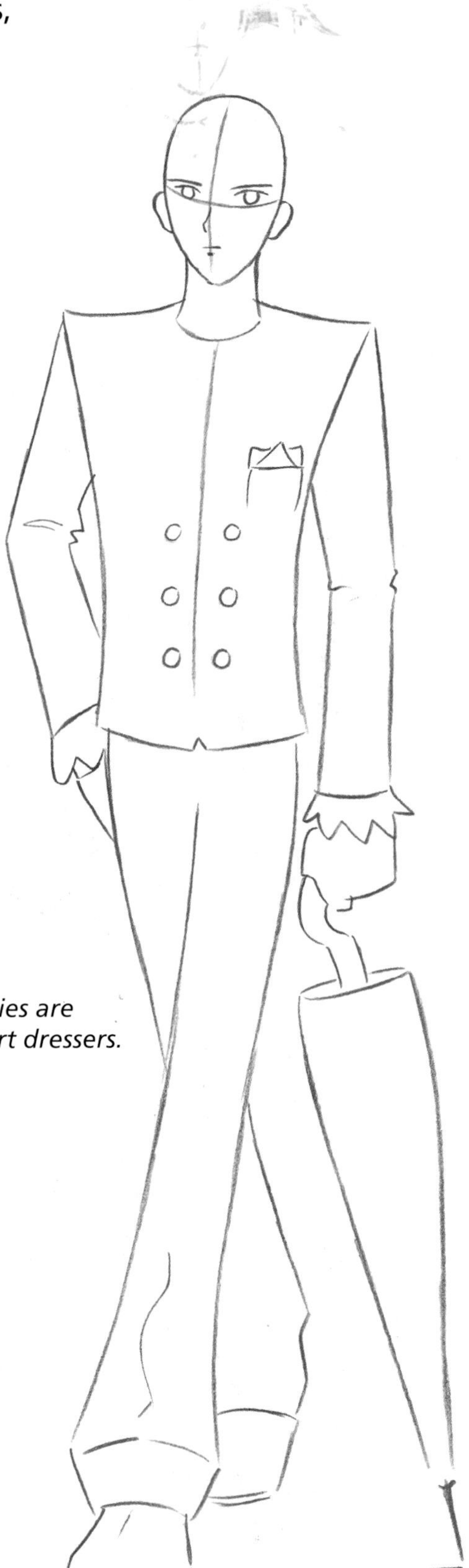

Bishies are smart dressers.

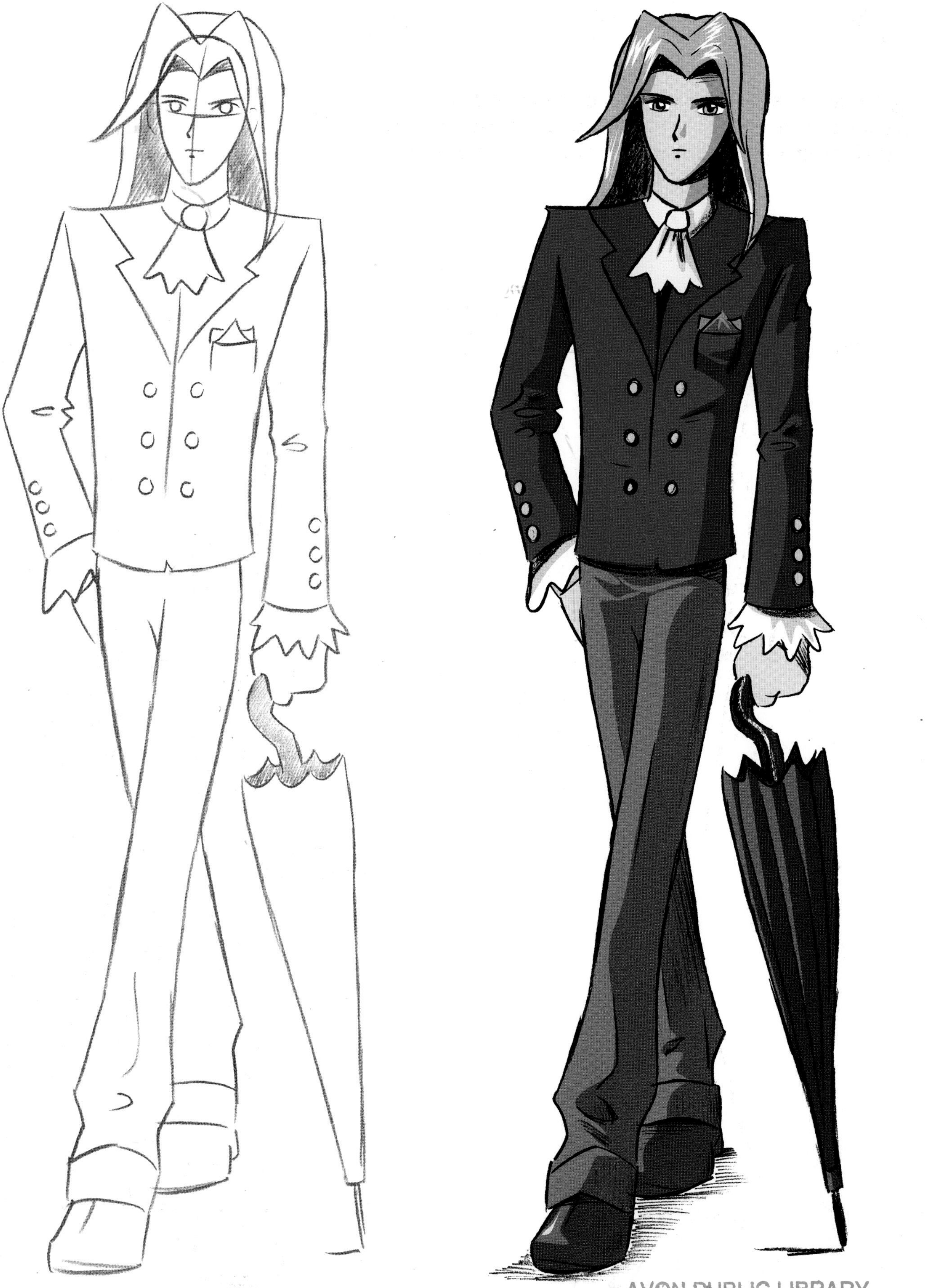

Drawing Seated Characters

The trick to drawing a character that's sitting down is to draw the chair first, *then* add the figure sitting on it. If you try to draw the character first, it will look weightless, as if the person is floating.

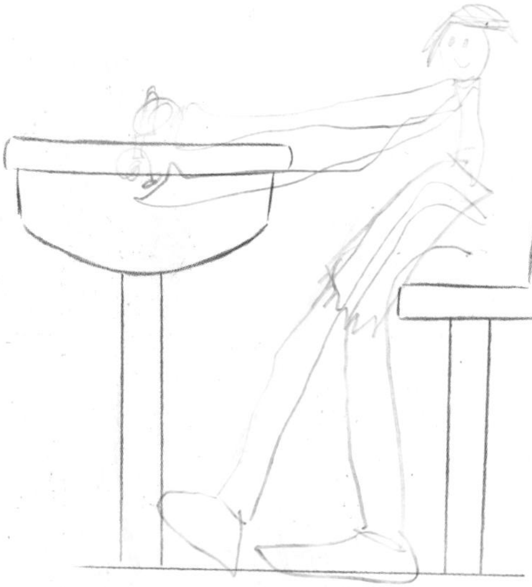

First draw the chair...

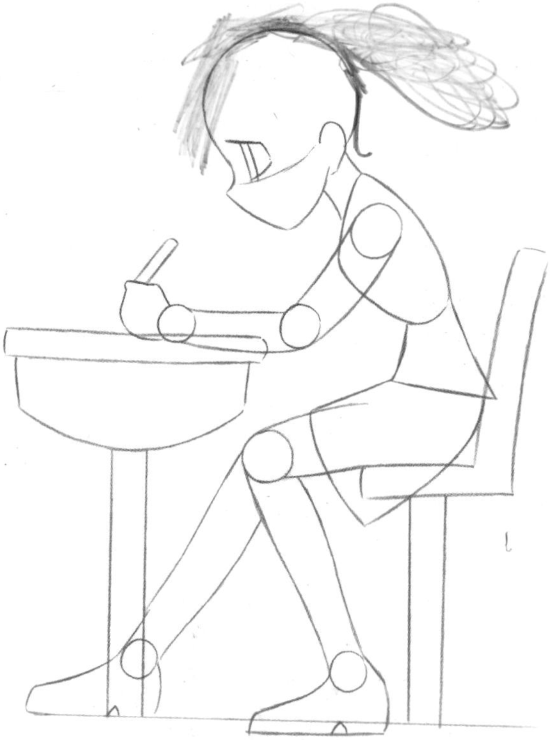

...then draw the girl sitting on the chair.

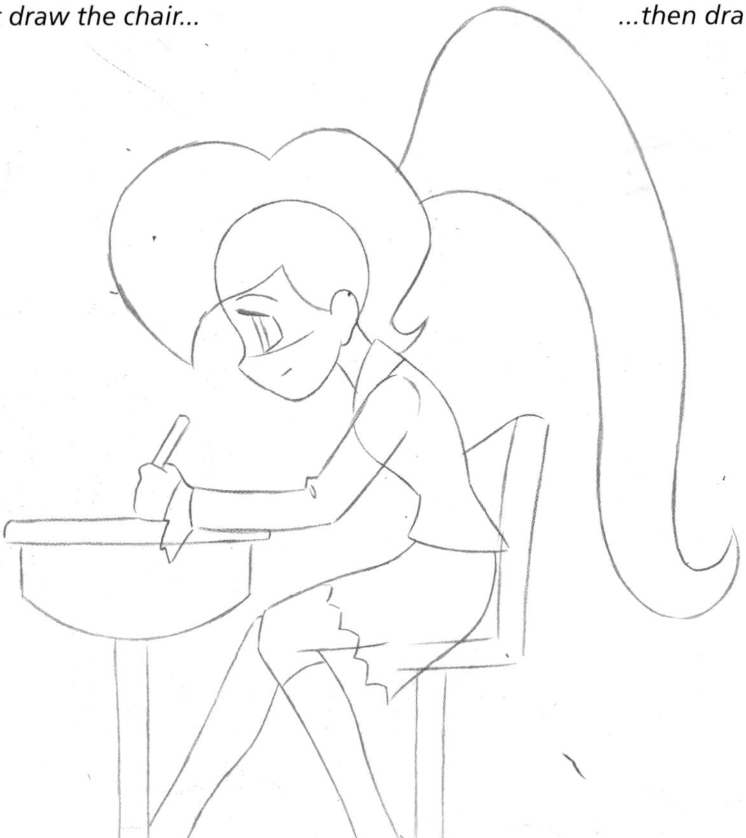

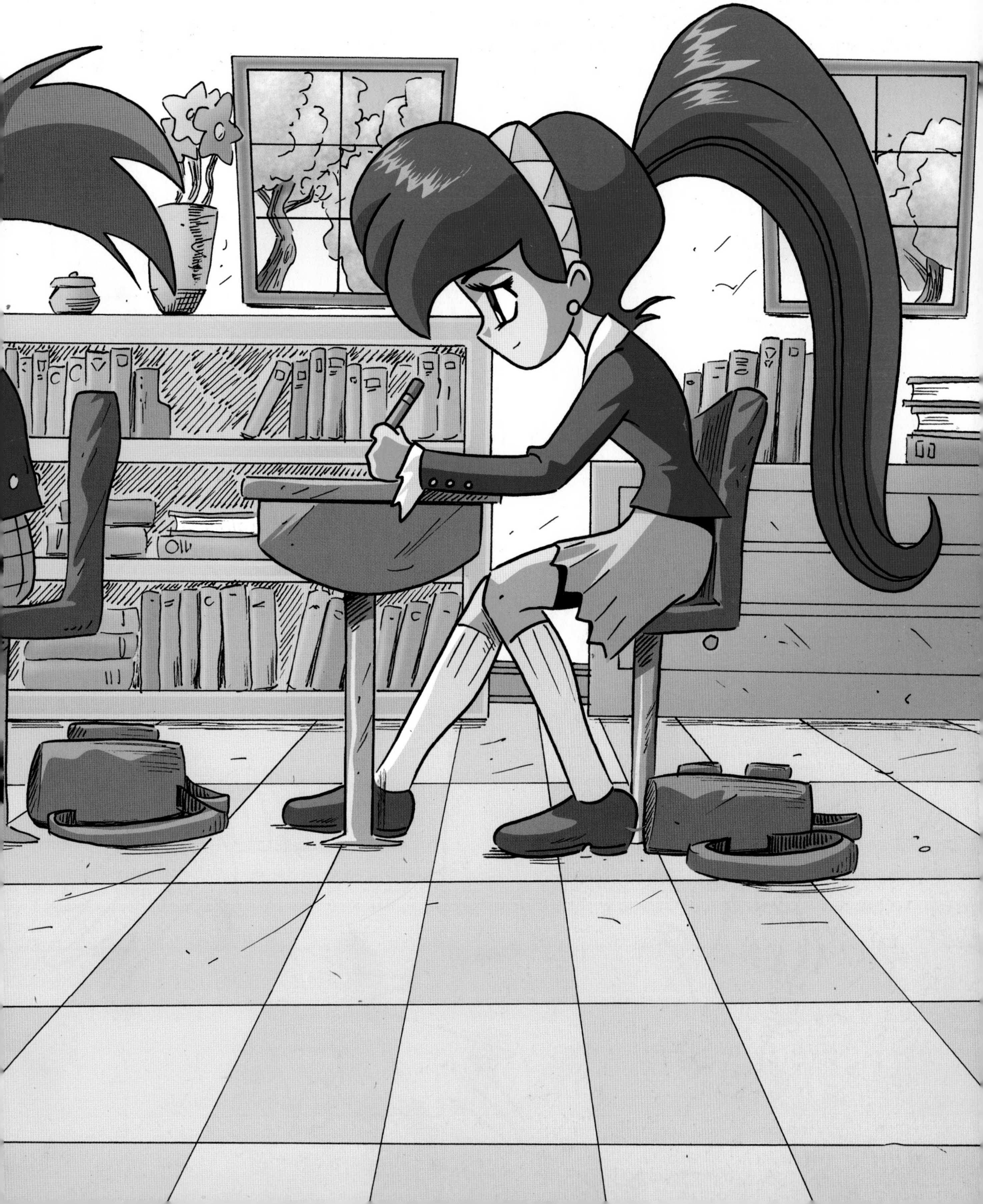

Drawing Hands

To draw real-looking hands, remember this: The knuckles and the fingers are drawn on an arch. Lightly sketch a curved line to help you draw the fingers and knuckles correctly.

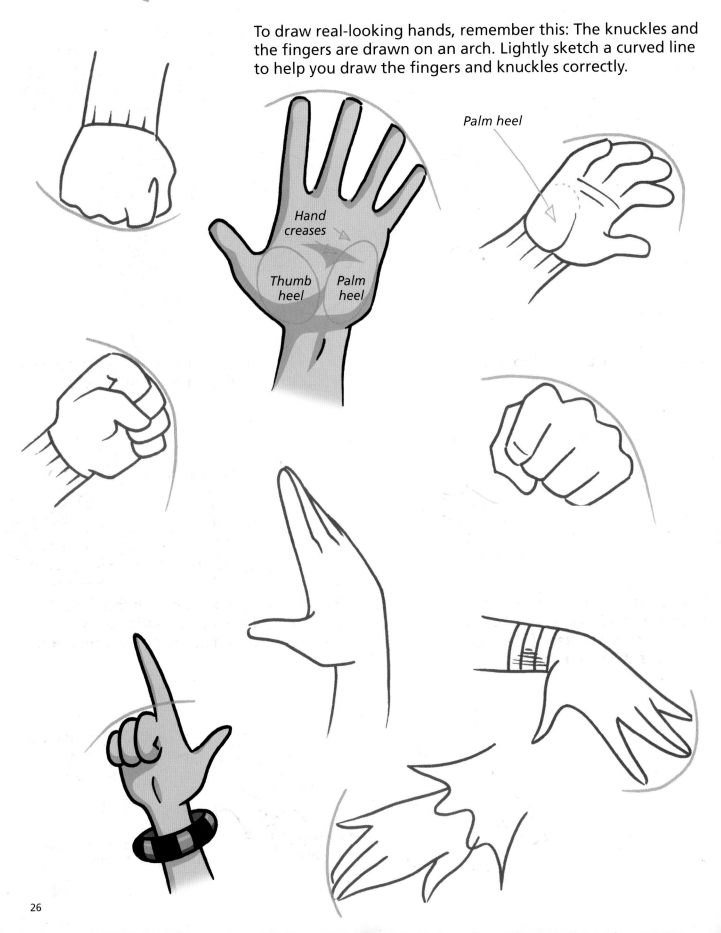

Palm heel

Hand creases

Thumb heel

Palm heel

Drawing Feet and Shoes

Feet are harder for people to draw than hands. Why? My guess is that people don't usually look at their own feet, but they always see and notice their own hands. Also, while the palm is almost flat, the foot has a built-in arch.

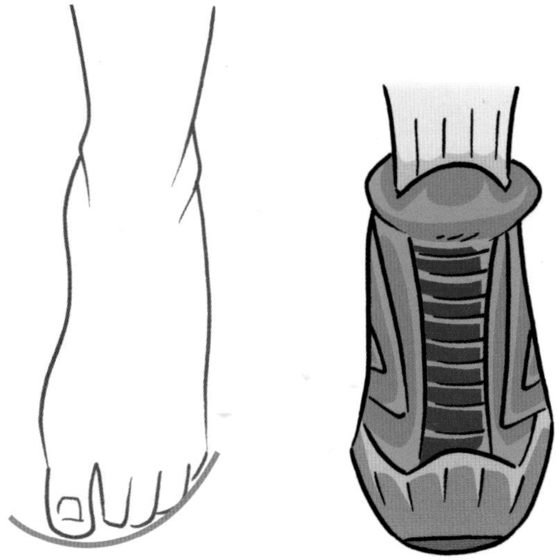

TOP VIEW
A shoe is shaped like a foot, but simpler.

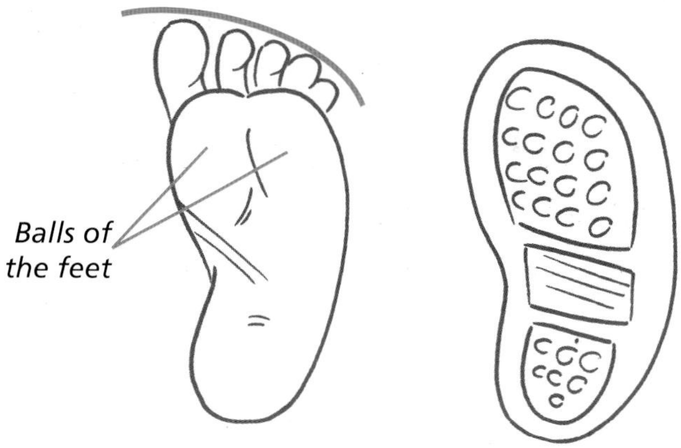
Balls of the feet

BOTTOM VIEW
Like fingers, toes follow a curve. The bottom of the sneaker should have grip marks.

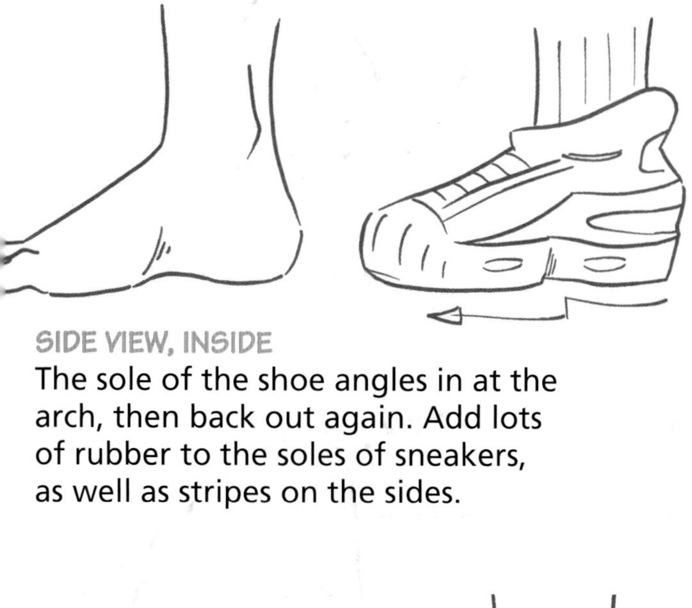

SIDE VIEW, INSIDE
The sole of the shoe angles in at the arch, then back out again. Add lots of rubber to the soles of sneakers, as well as stripes on the sides.

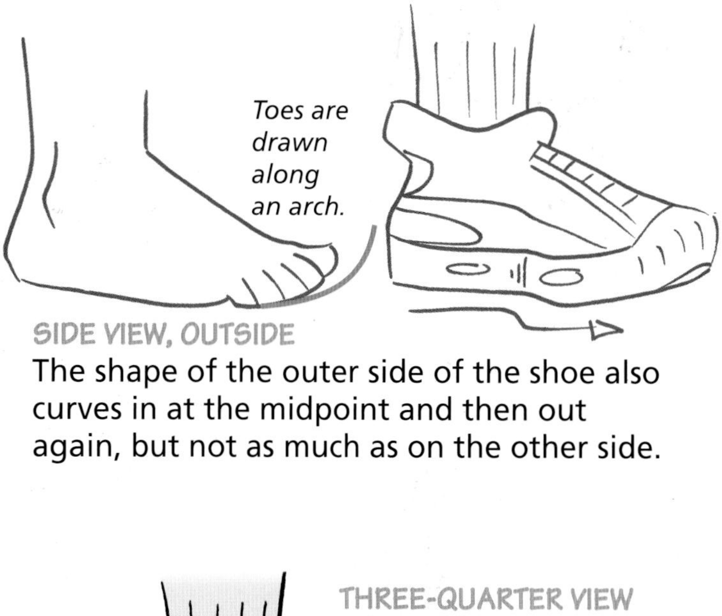
Toes are drawn along an arch.

SIDE VIEW, OUTSIDE
The shape of the outer side of the shoe also curves in at the midpoint and then out again, but not as much as on the other side.

THREE-QUARTER VIEW
In this view, you should see a little bit of the bottom of the sole.

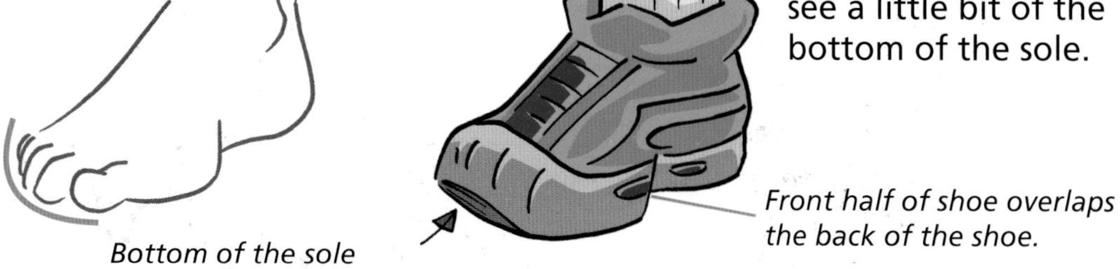
Bottom of the sole
Front half of shoe overlaps the back of the shoe.

SCHOOL COMICS

Now that you've mastered the basics, it's time for the exciting part: creating great characters! Let's start with school comics, which focus on the adventures of school-age teens, and are among the most popular types of shoujo. If you can draw the core characters, you're on your way to creating your own comics!

Uniforms for Girls

First, let's look at school uniforms. In the United States, kids in school wear jeans, T-shirts, whatever they like. But in Japan, girls and boys are required to wear uniforms. So shoujo characters wear these outfits in school...but after school, and on weekends, they can wear anything they like. Here are some typical uniforms for girls. Skirts are just above the knee, and shirts have high necklines.

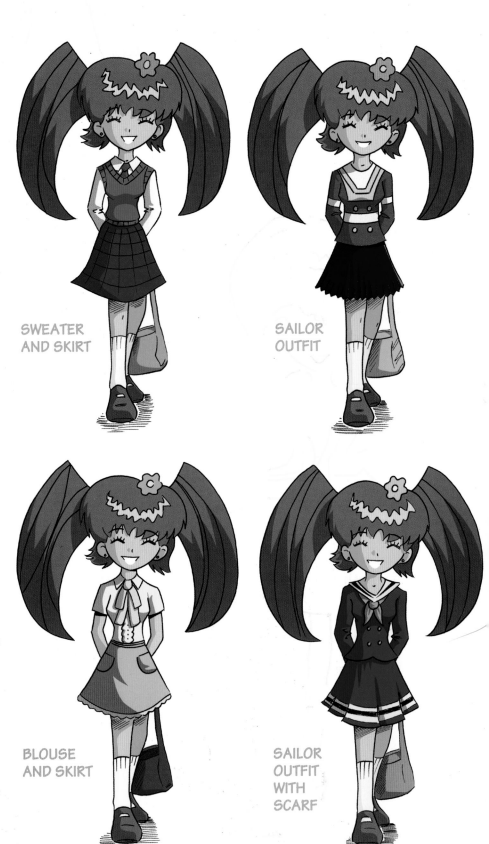

SWEATER AND SKIRT

SAILOR OUTFIT

BLOUSE AND SKIRT

SAILOR OUTFIT WITH SCARF

Uniforms for Boys

Boys' uniforms can be a simple suit, a neat sweater and trousers, or a trendy jacket and pants.

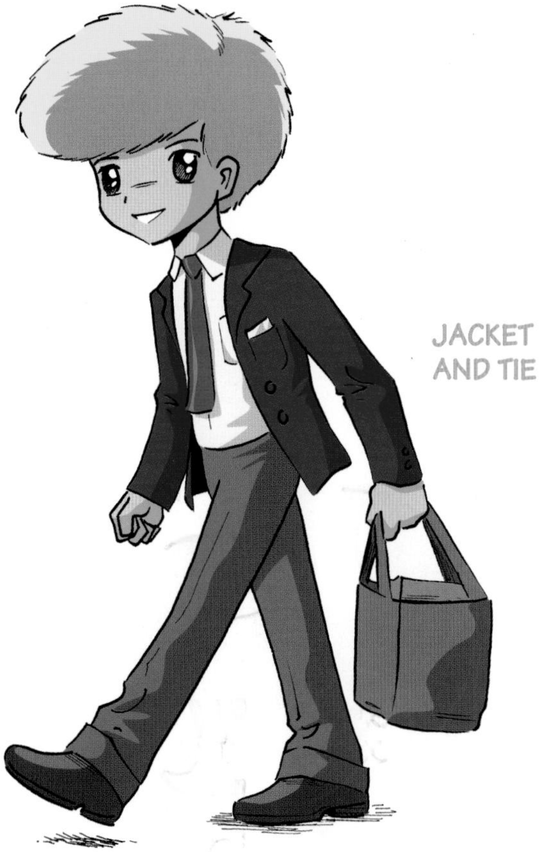
JACKET
AND TIE

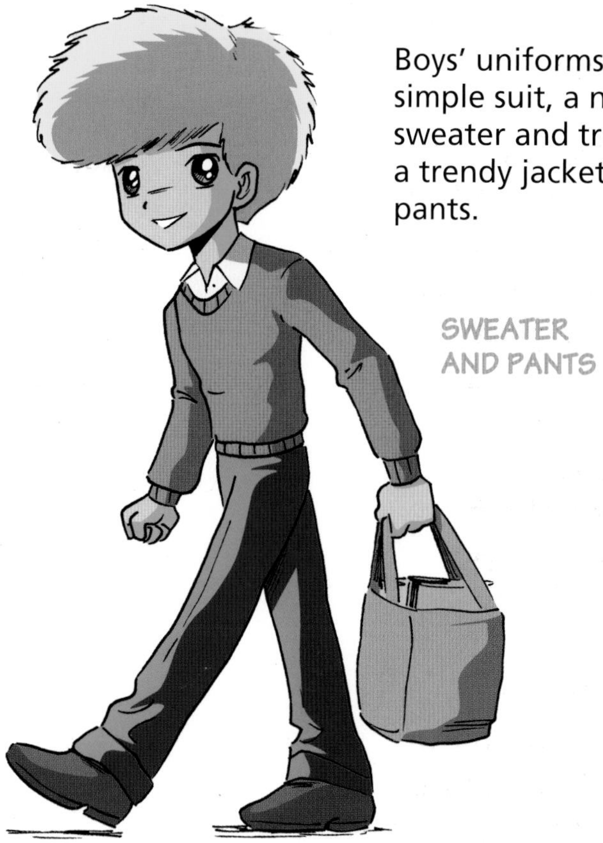
SWEATER
AND PANTS

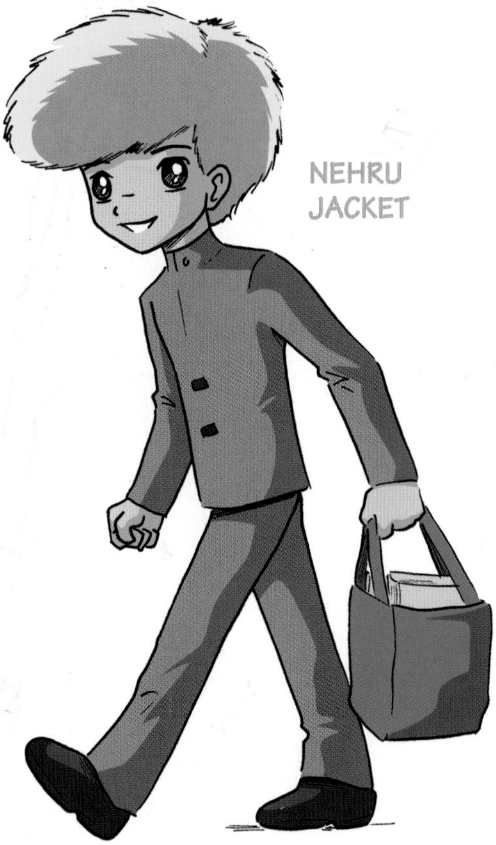
NEHRU
JACKET

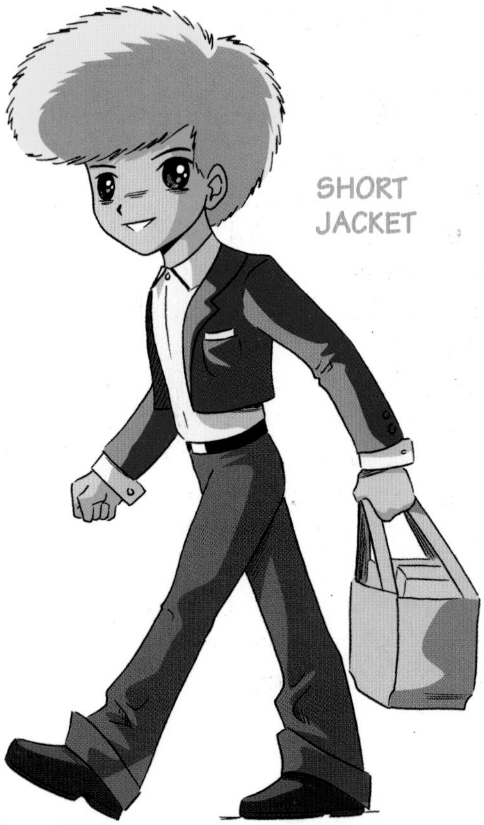
SHORT
JACKET

Student Athlete

A student athlete is a staple of school comics. You don't have to draw fancy moves or extreme poses—all that's needed is a team uniform, athletic shoes, and a ball.

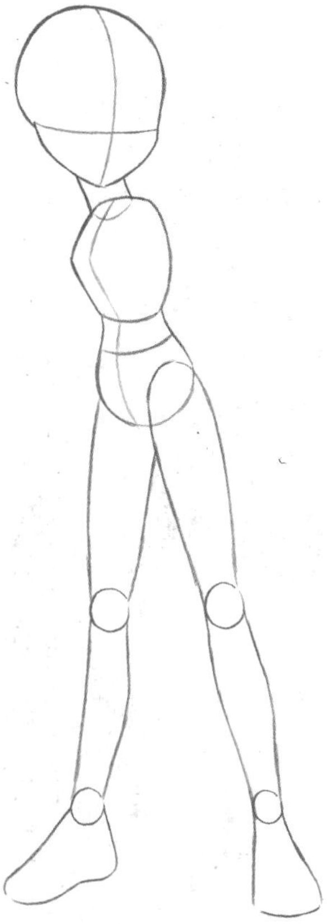

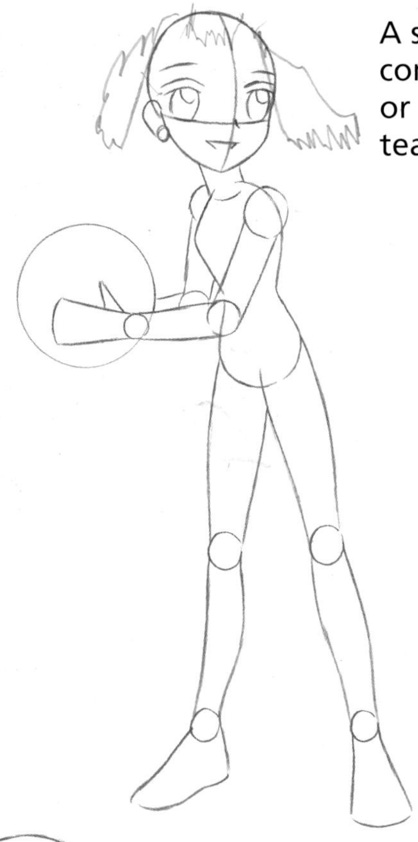

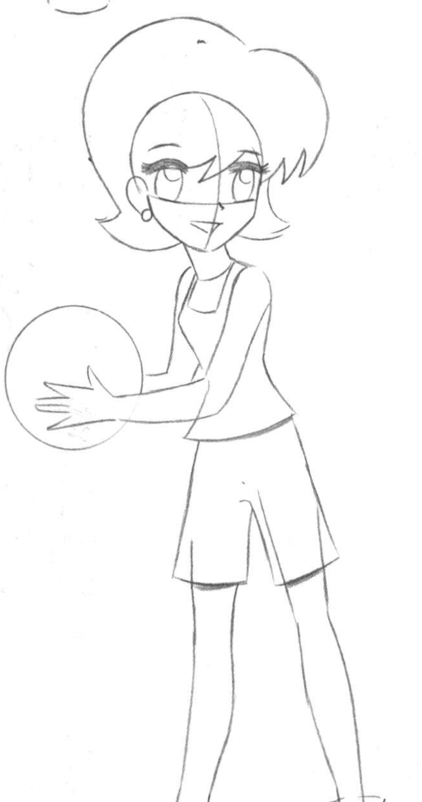

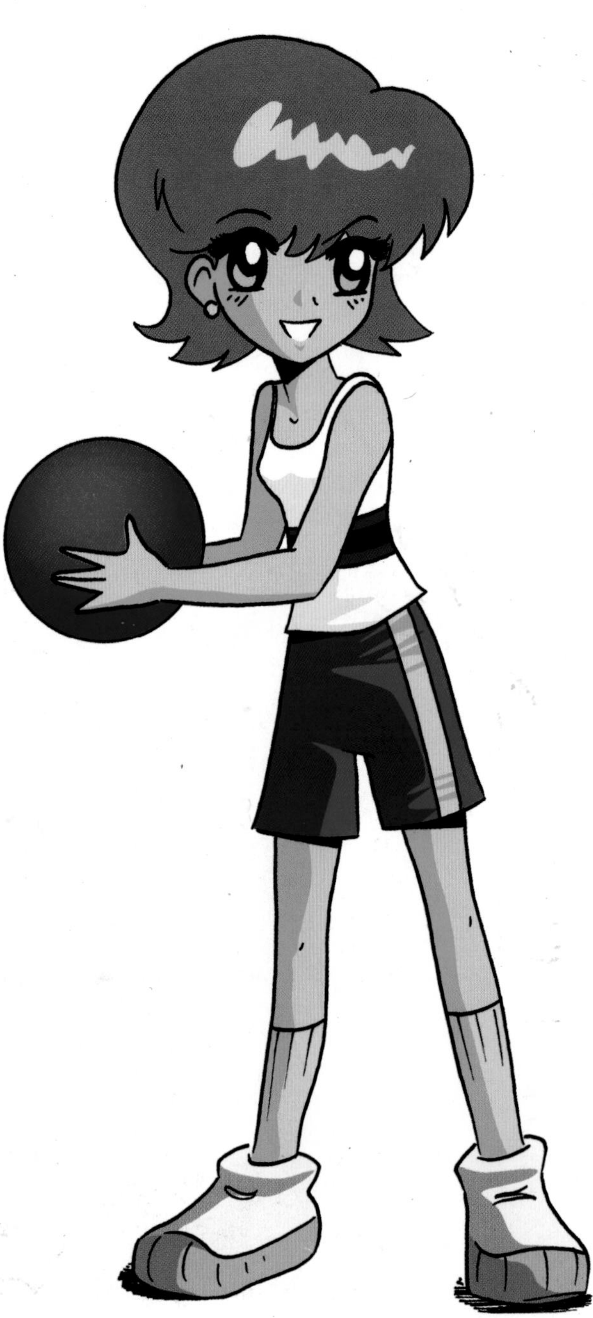

Cheerful Teen

Here's a bright-eyed teenager with a big smile. In shoujo, a popular look is to leave the open mouth blank, without showing the teeth or tongue.

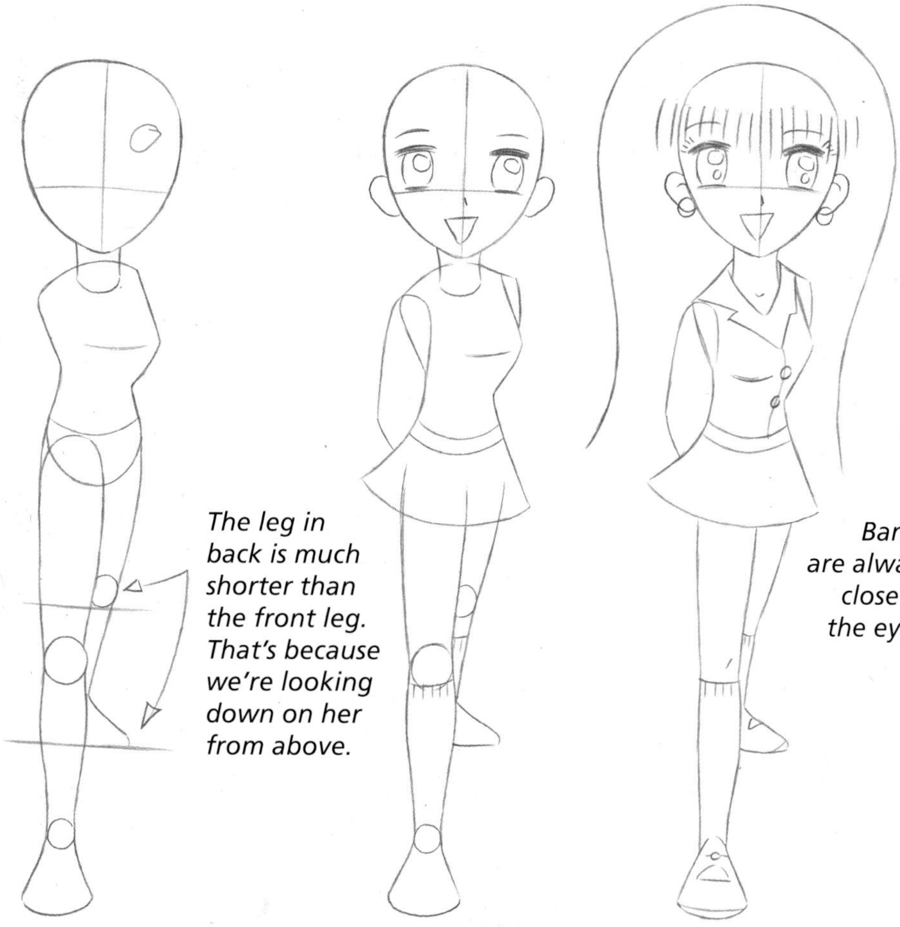
The leg in back is much shorter than the front leg. That's because we're looking down on her from above.

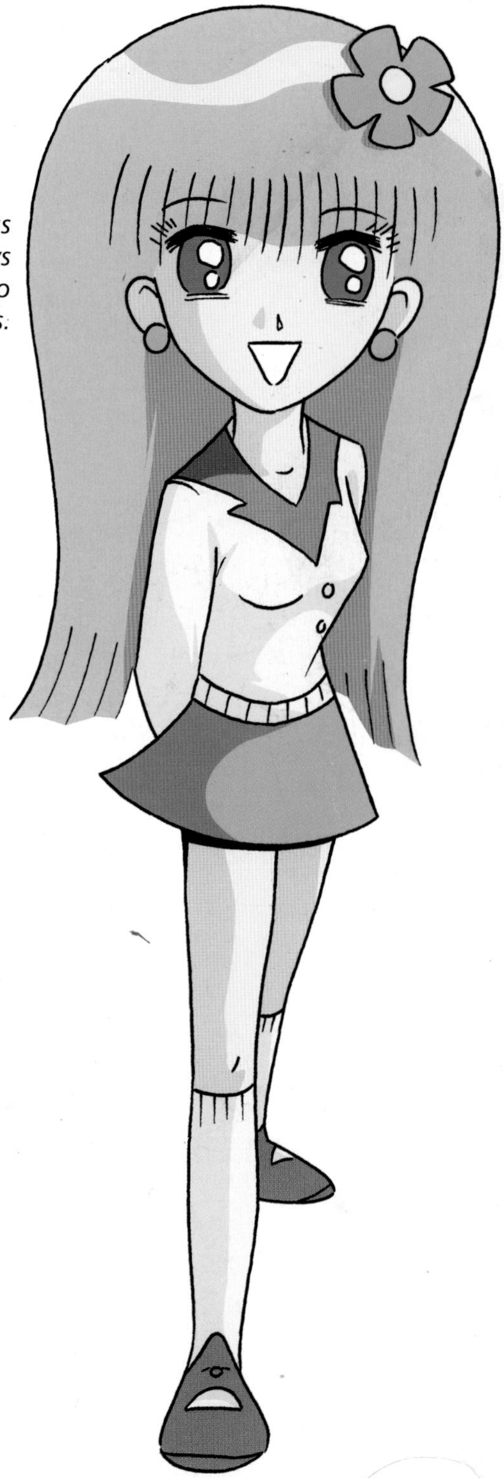
Bangs are always close to the eyes.

BOWS, JEWELS, AND FLOWERS

Shoujo artists like to embellish their work with graceful decorations. Here are some extras you can use for your characters.

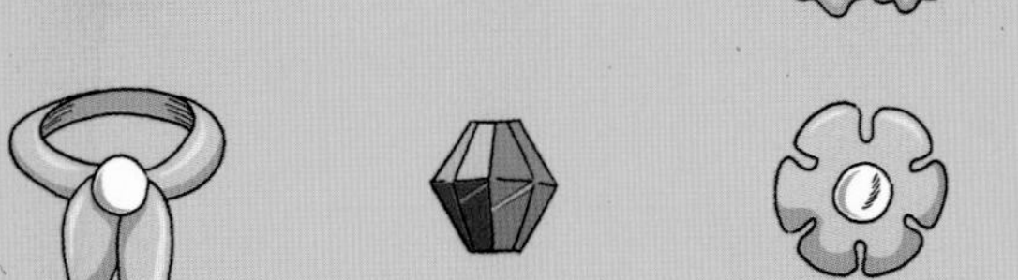

Joe Cool

Okay, so he's vain and self-centered. Readers still love characters like this, and so do all of the schoolgirl characters in shoujo! Note the stylish crew-neck shirt with the open jacket—very trendy.

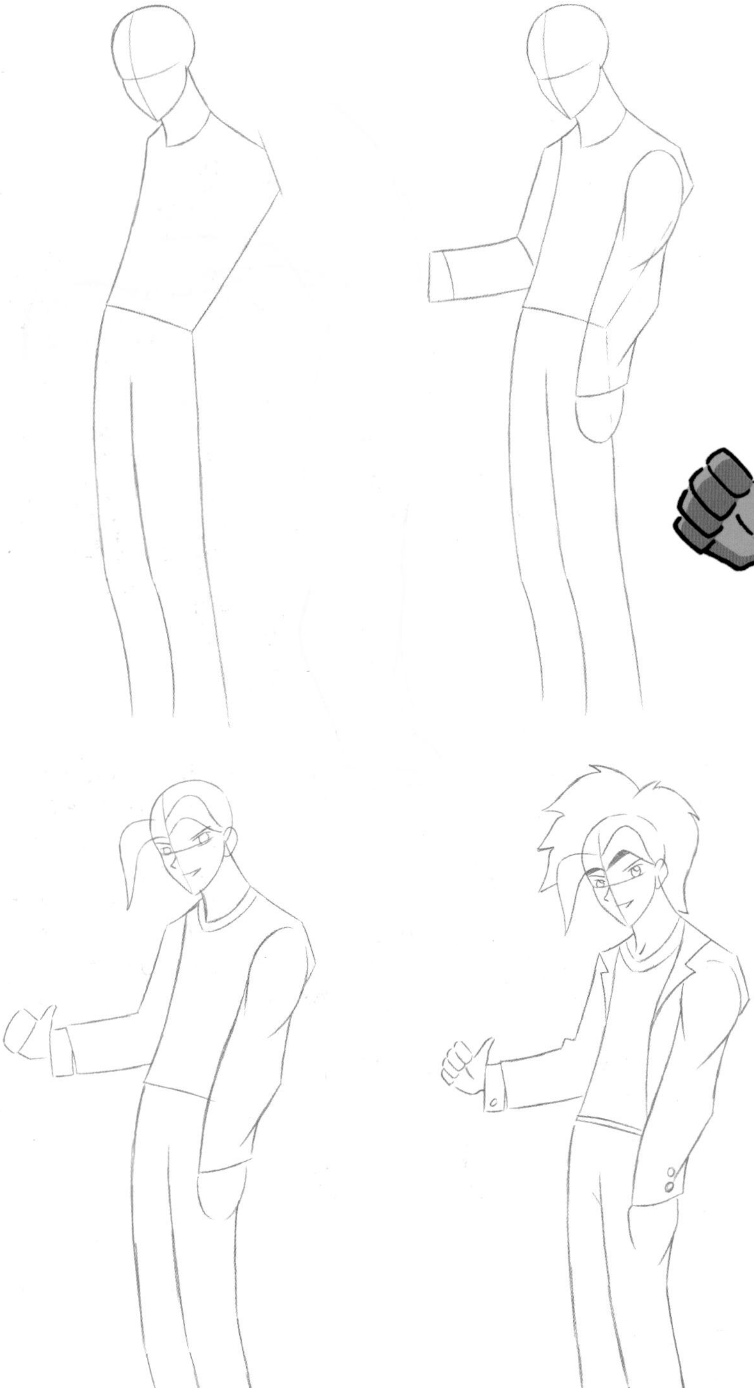

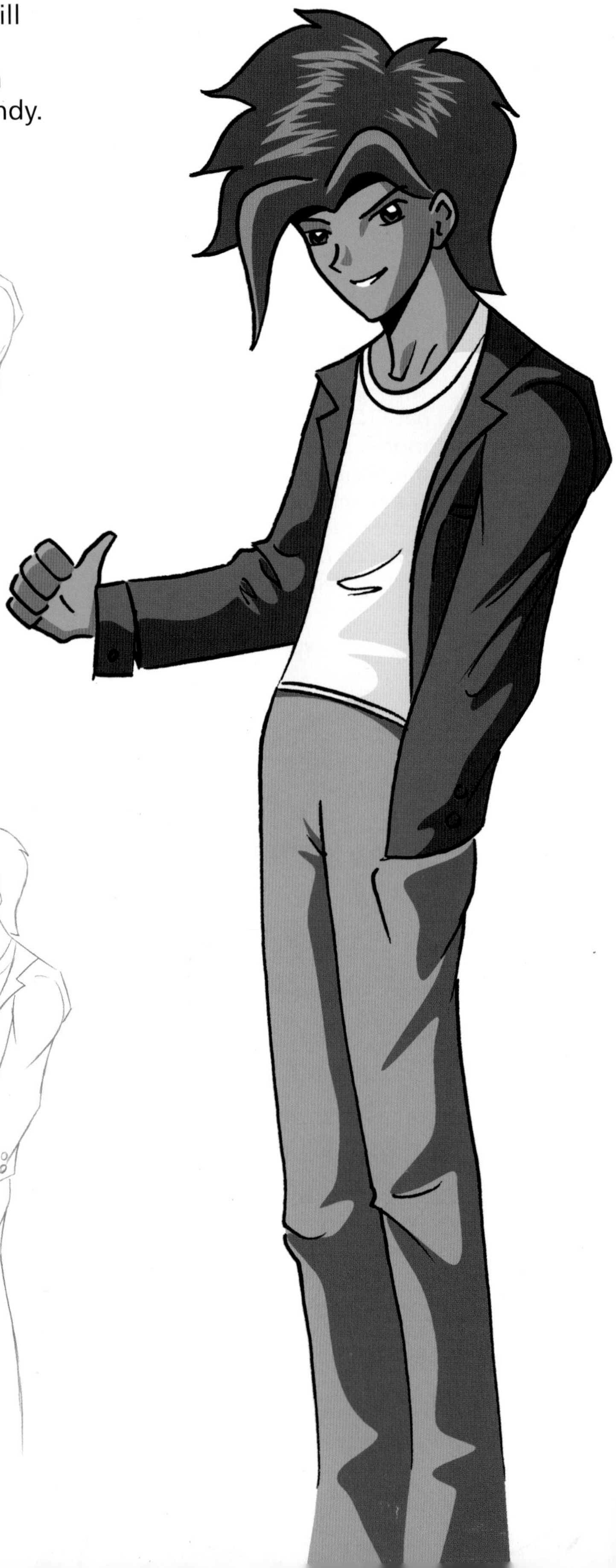

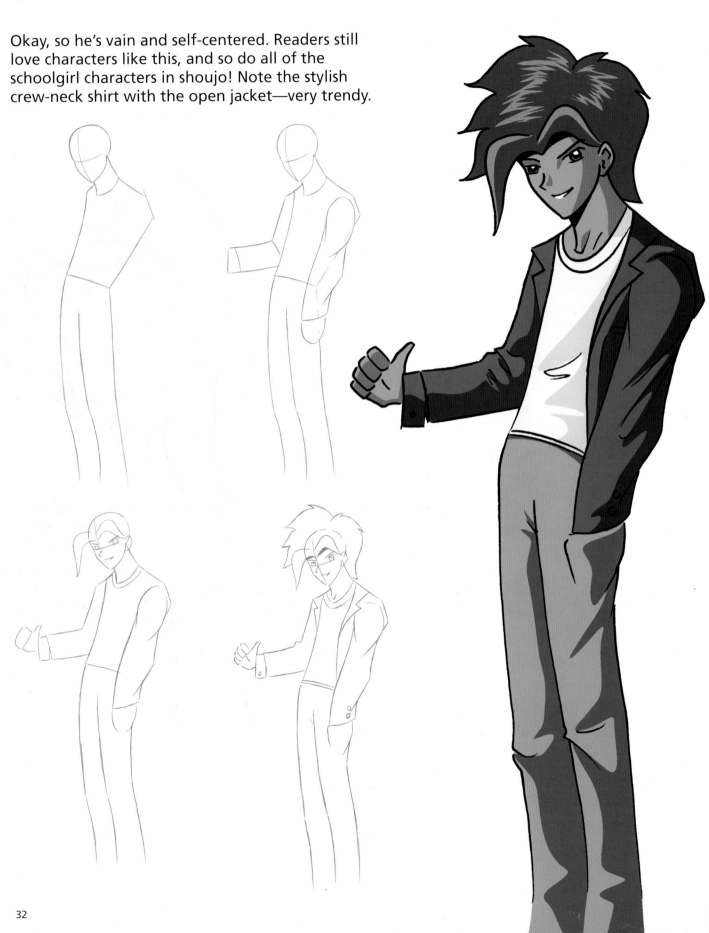

Teen Idol

All the girls are crazy about this type of character. There's always one of these popular types in every school. And in my school, it was me (just kidding!). Give the teen idol character a well-defined jaw and chin. Don't make his face too round—he should look a little older than the other kids.

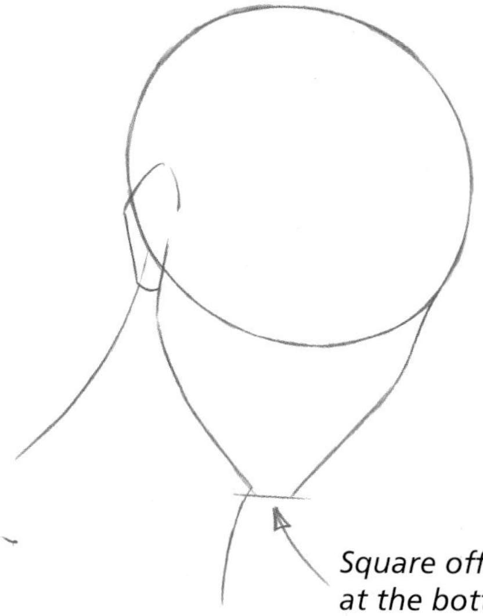

Square off the chin at the bottom.

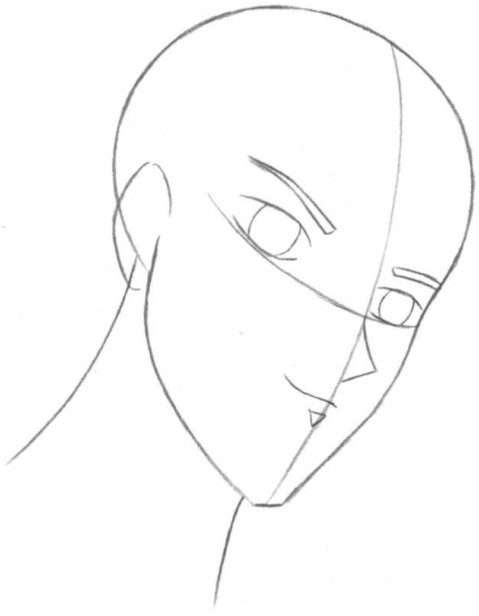

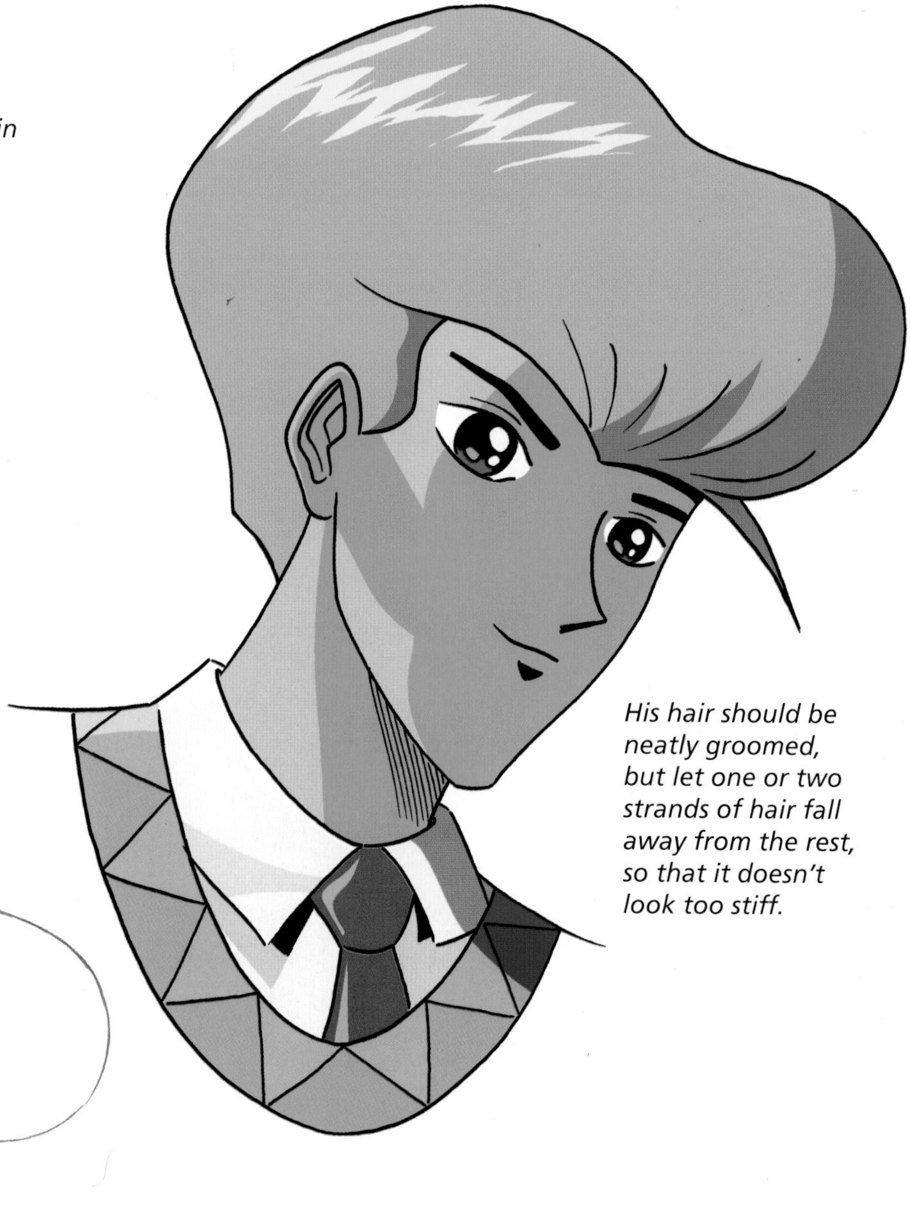

His hair should be neatly groomed, but let one or two strands of hair fall away from the rest, so that it doesn't look too stiff.

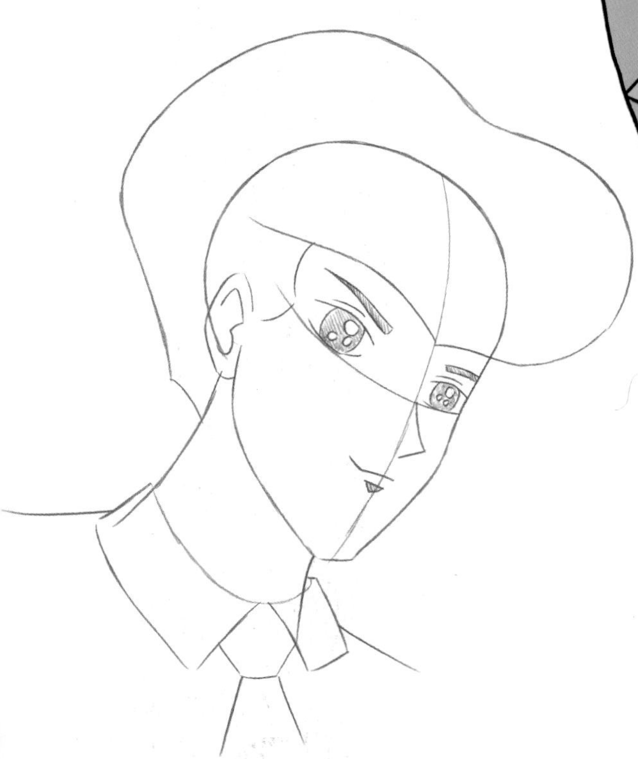

Lunch Break

Time for a picnic lunch. To create a casual mood, this schoolboy's jacket is open and the sleeves are rolled up. His crossed legs are easy to draw, because you don't have to show his feet!

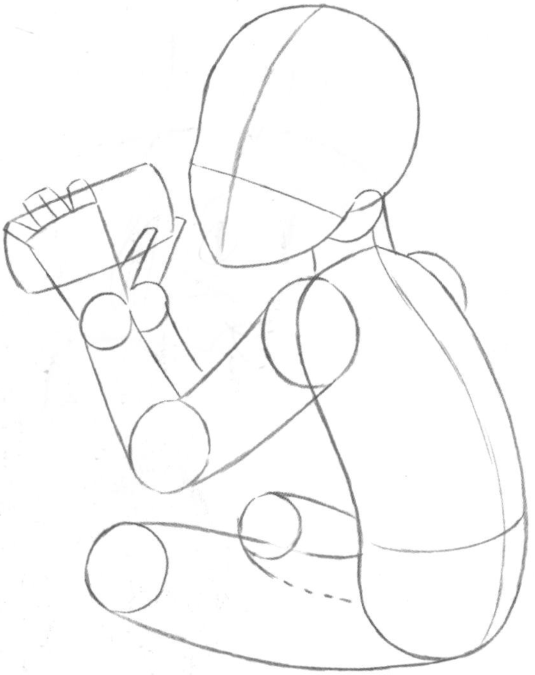

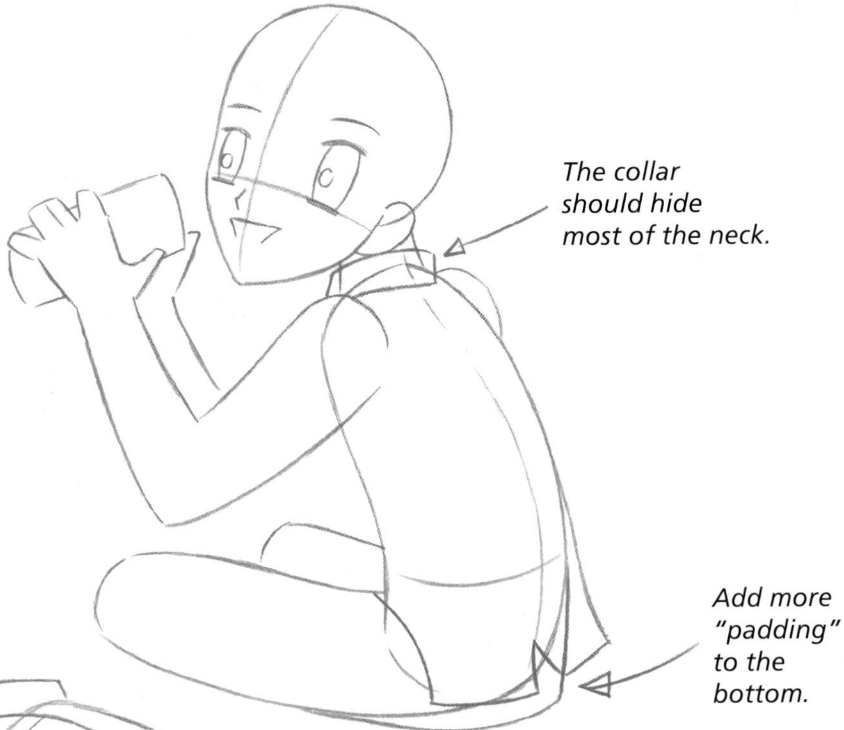
The collar should hide most of the neck.
Add more "padding" to the bottom.

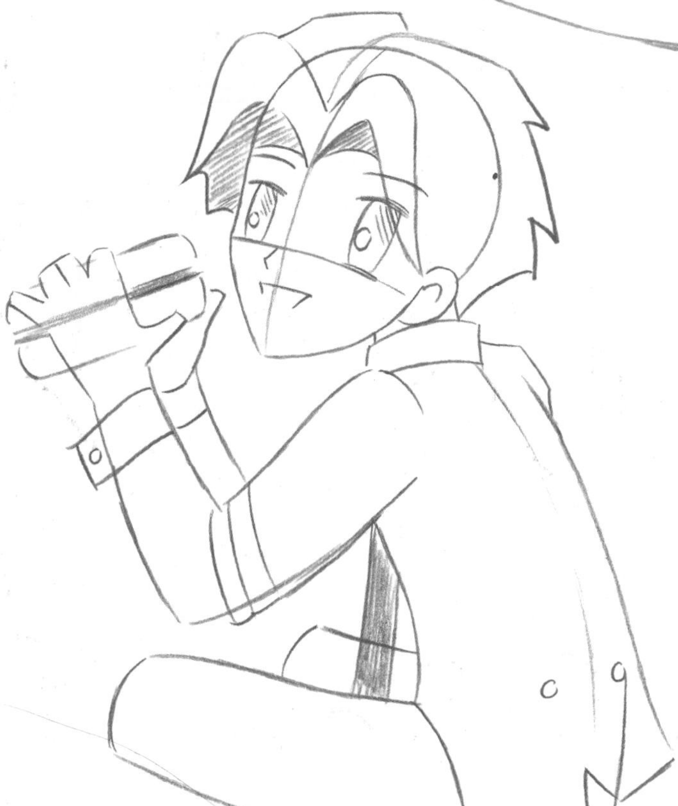

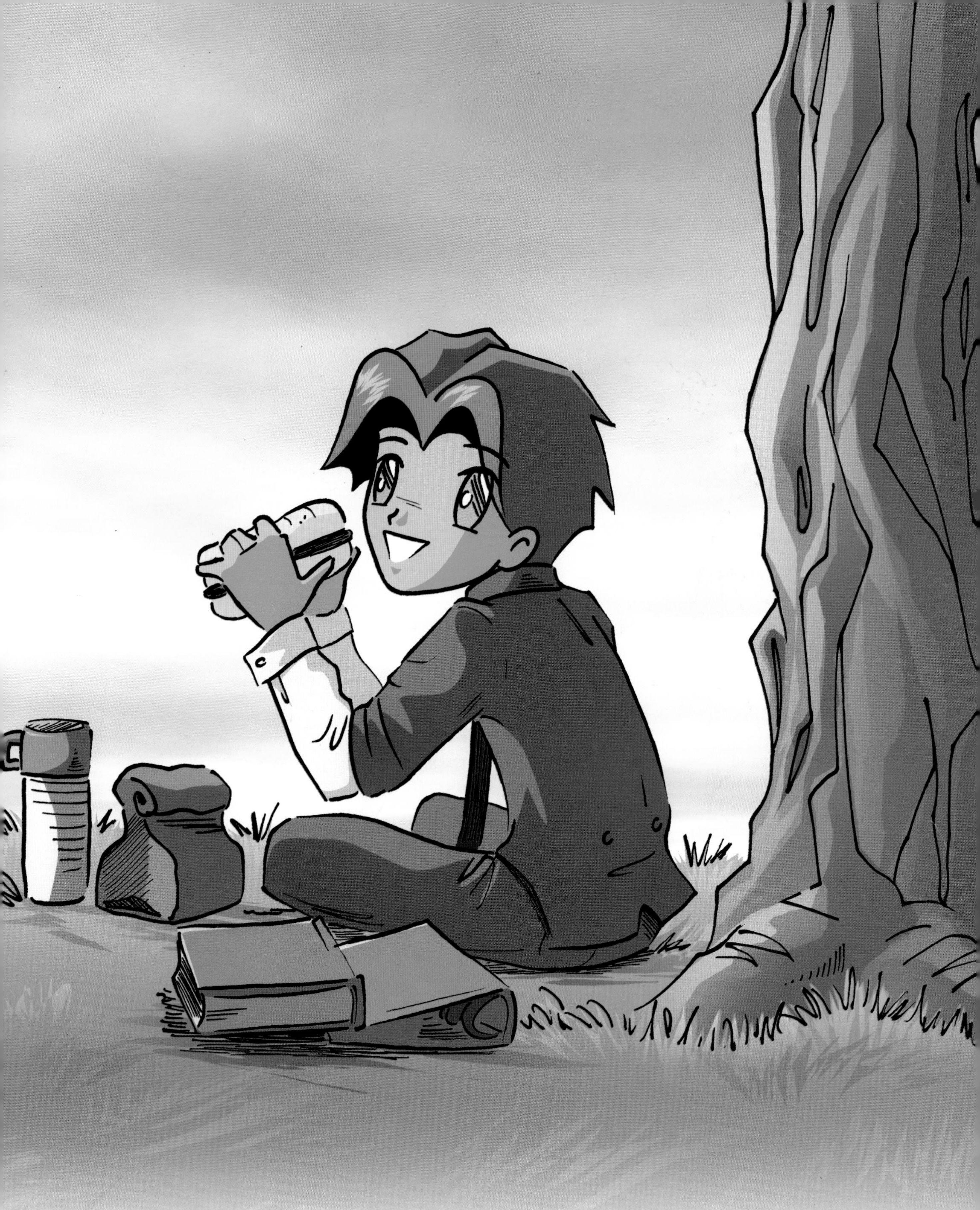

Backpack Boy

Nehru jackets are popular, and since the shape of the jacket is basically a rectangle, you can just draw a rectangle for the upper body. Easy! The trademark of the Nehru jacket is the high collar. Give the boy a center part and wild hair sticking up from the back.

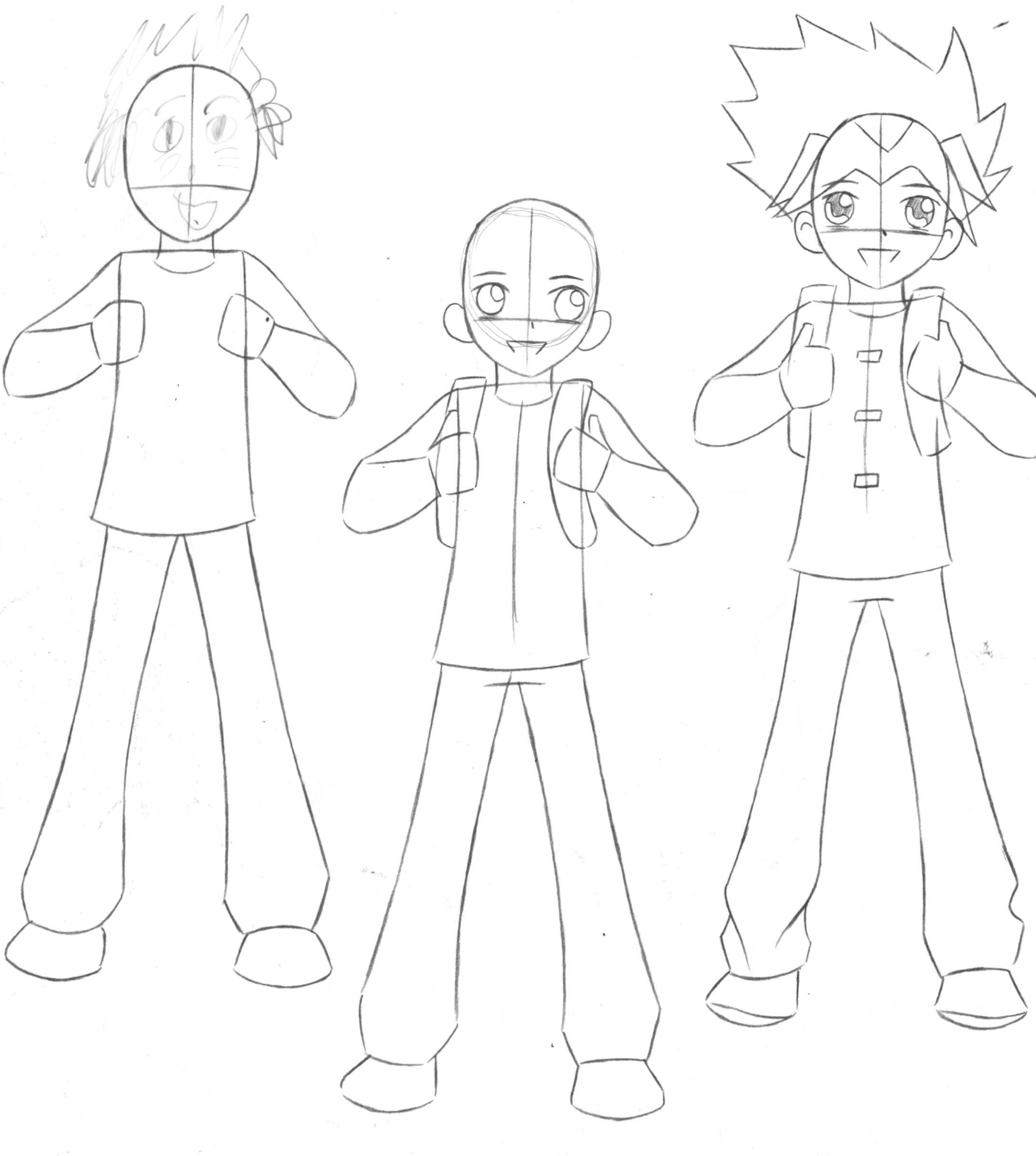

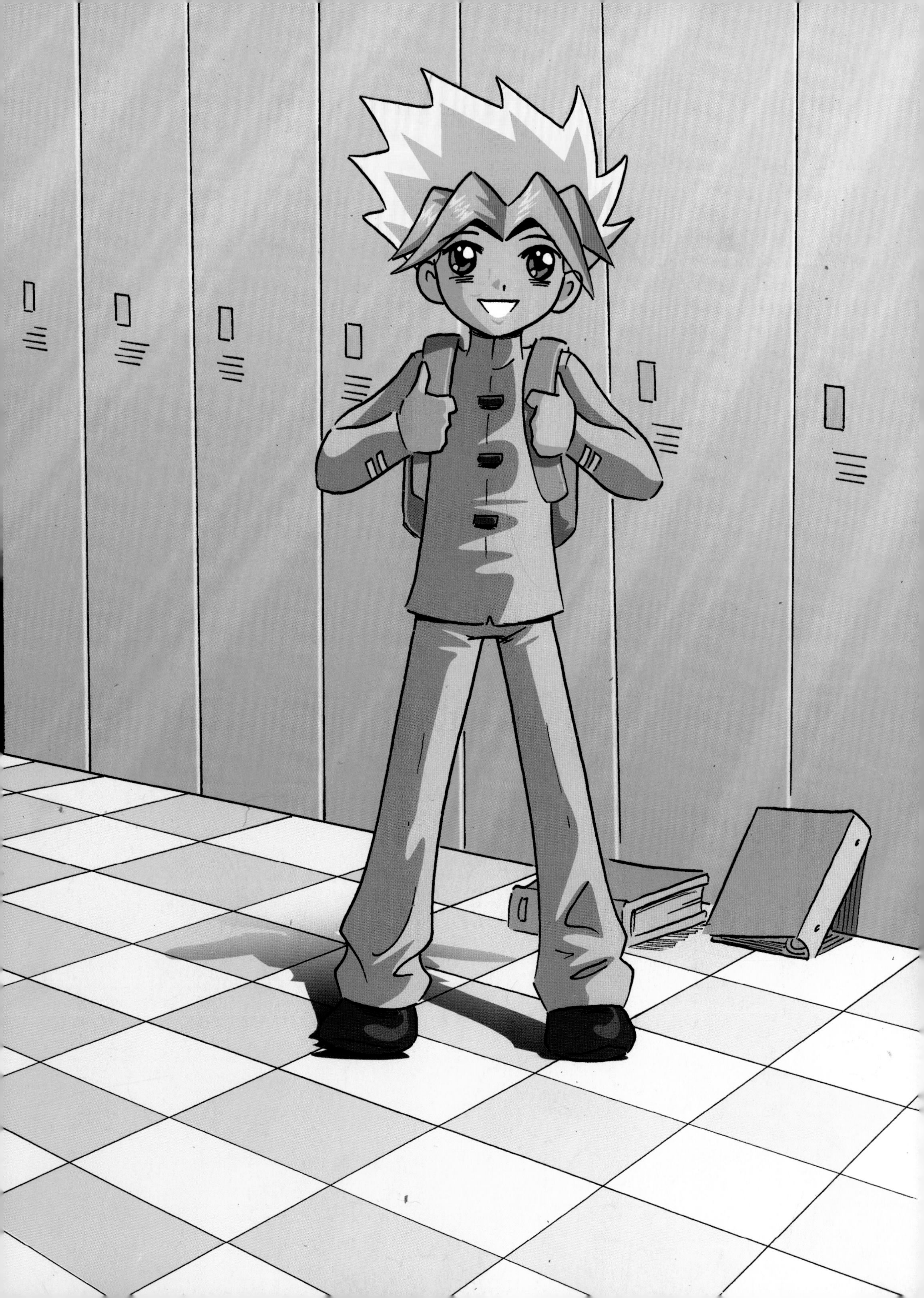

Sidewalk Racer

See how the pose makes her look as if she's really riding the skateboard? What makes this pose so convincing? The arms? They're important—but the key is the way she's bending her knees in. Also, she bends a bit at the waist. In action poses, the worst thing you can do is make your character stiff. Keep her loose and flexible!

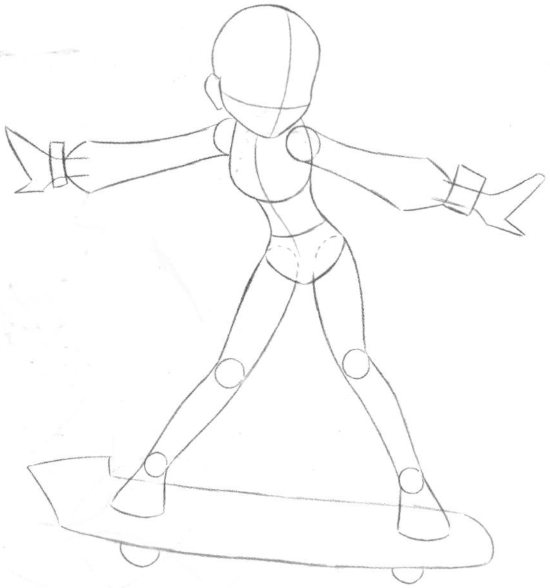

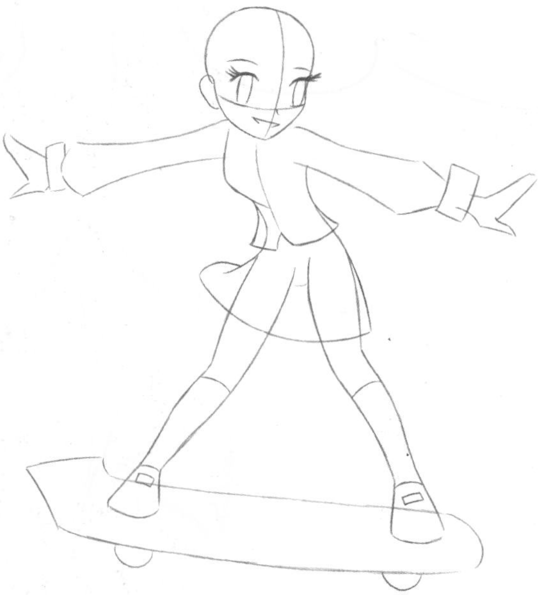

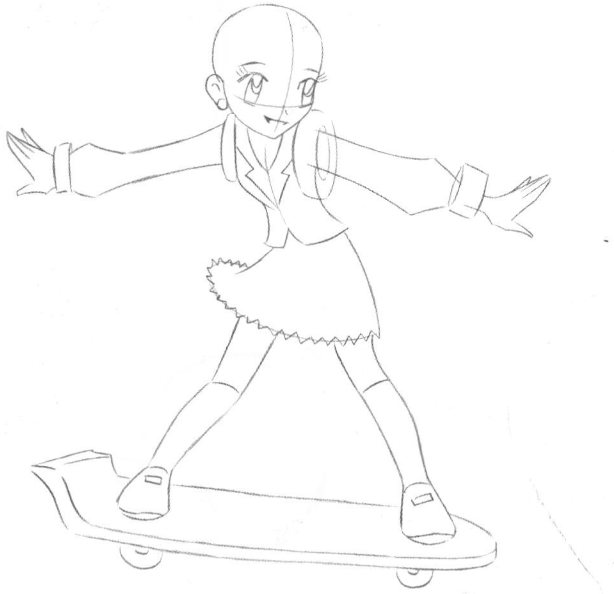

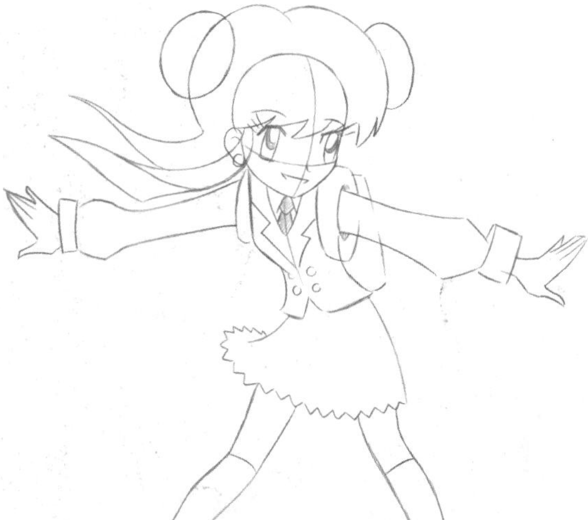

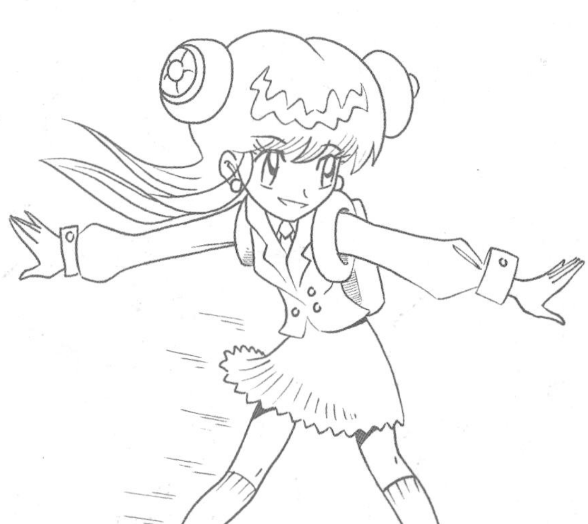

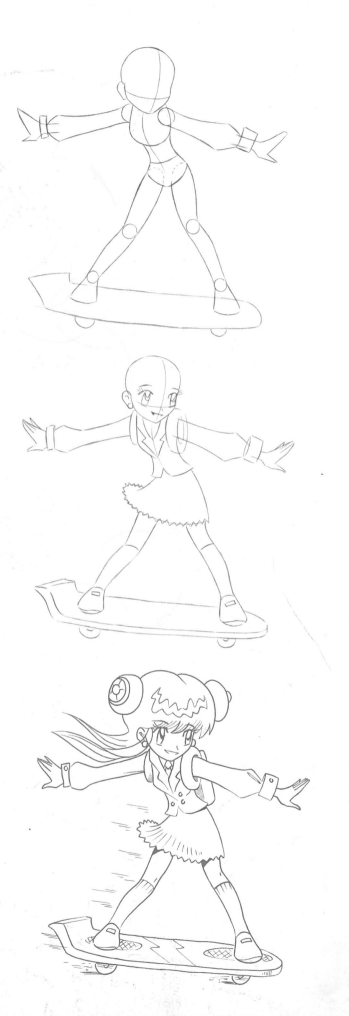

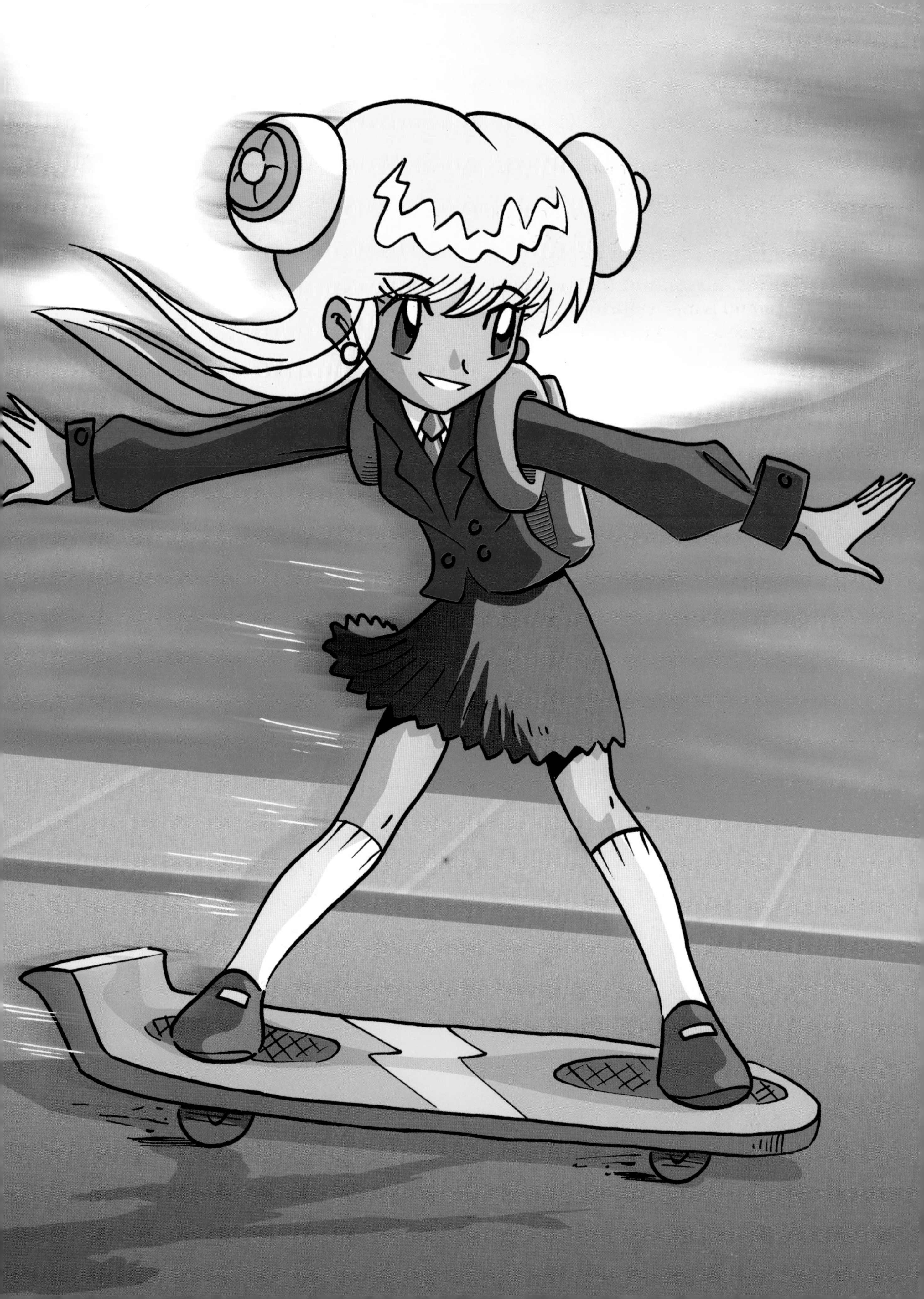

MAGIC TIME

Some of the coolest characters in shoujo are the beings with special powers—magical girls and boys, goddesses and demigods, fantasy fighters, princesses, fairies, elves, and many more. Learning to draw these characters will add excitement to your manga shoujo!

Magical Girls

Magical girls take school comics one step further. Most of the time, these characters are ordinary schoolgirls. But when faced with injustice and evil, they use secret powers to transform themselves into powerful fighters to defeat the forces of darkness. Their costumes are often based on school uniforms.

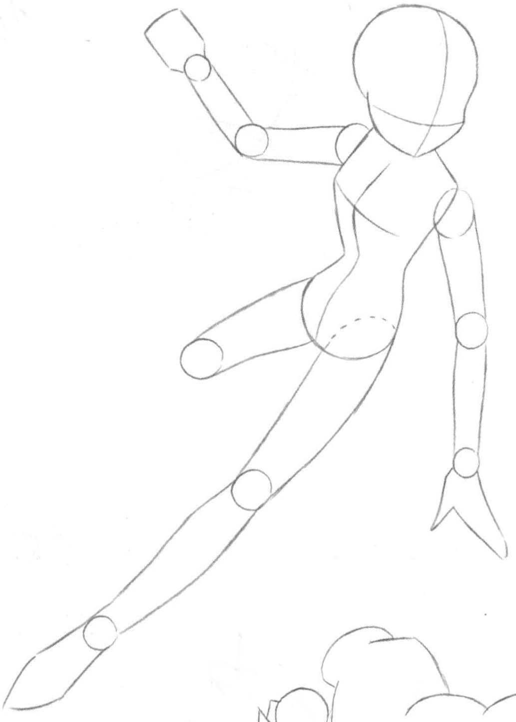

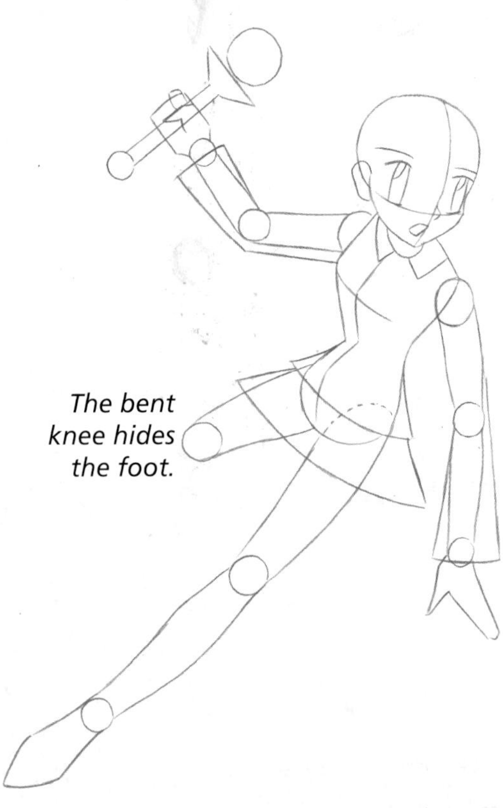

The bent knee hides the foot.

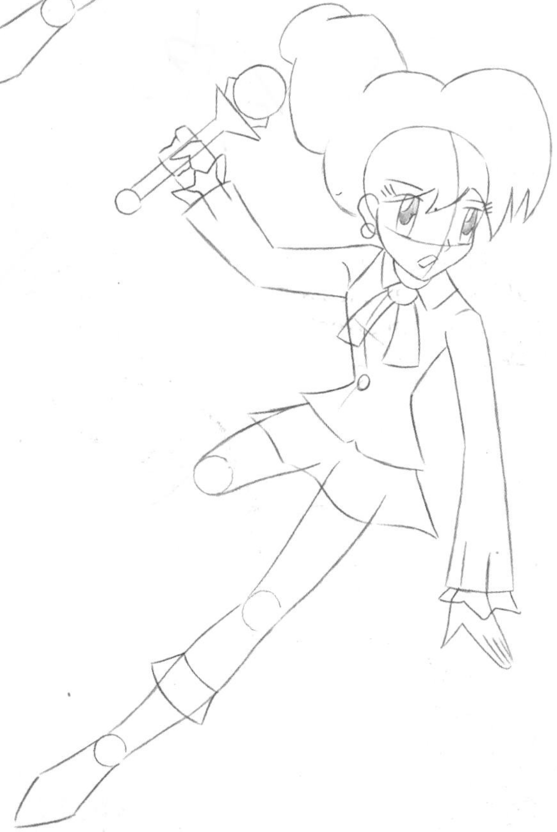

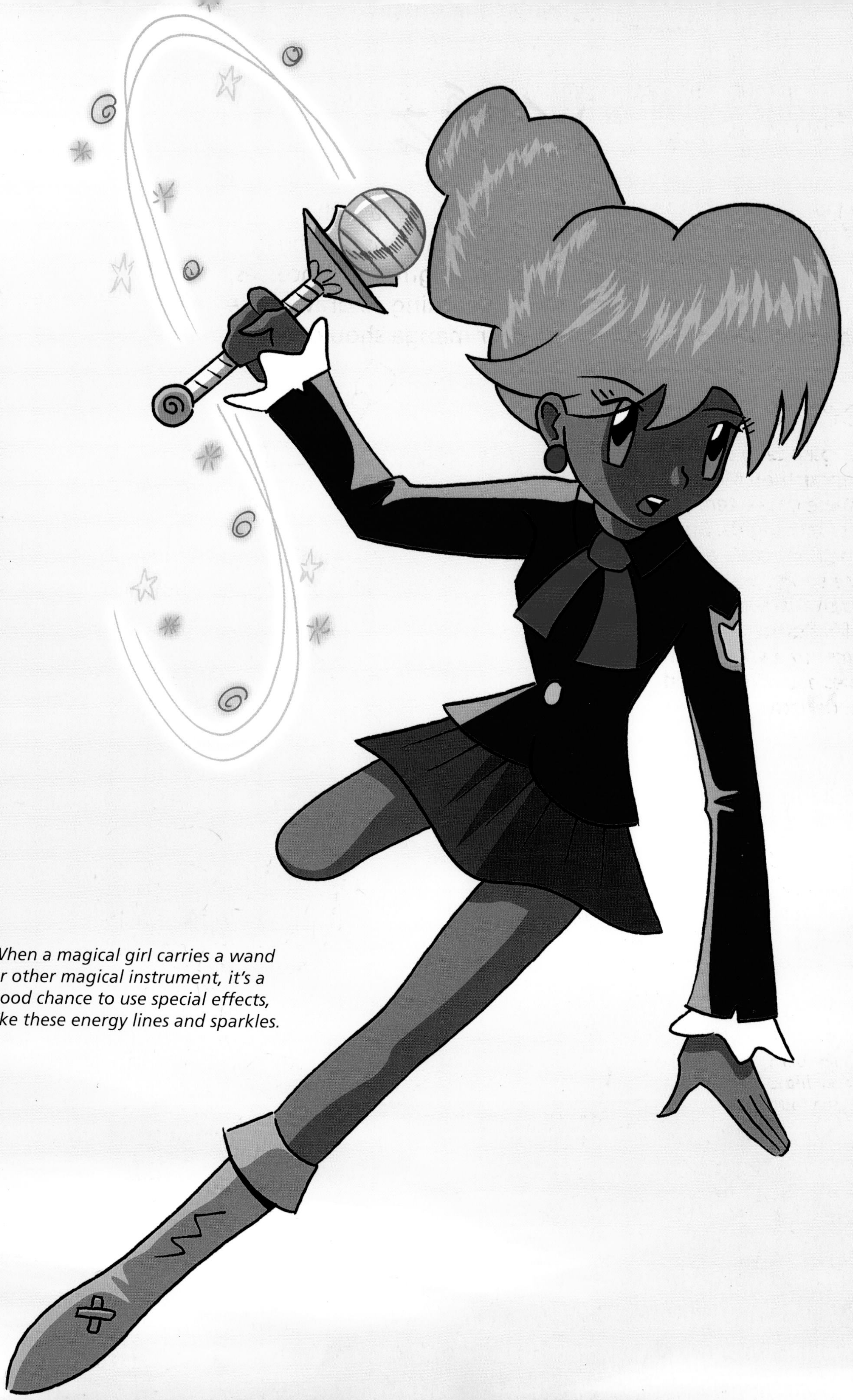

When a magical girl carries a wand or other magical instrument, it's a good chance to use special effects, like these energy lines and sparkles.

Magical Girl with Cape

Here's a fancy magical girl character. To make it easy, I've broken it down into six simple steps. The hair, in the last step, makes it look hard. But actually, that's the easiest part—you can draw the hair differently than I do, and it will be a hairstyle you invented!

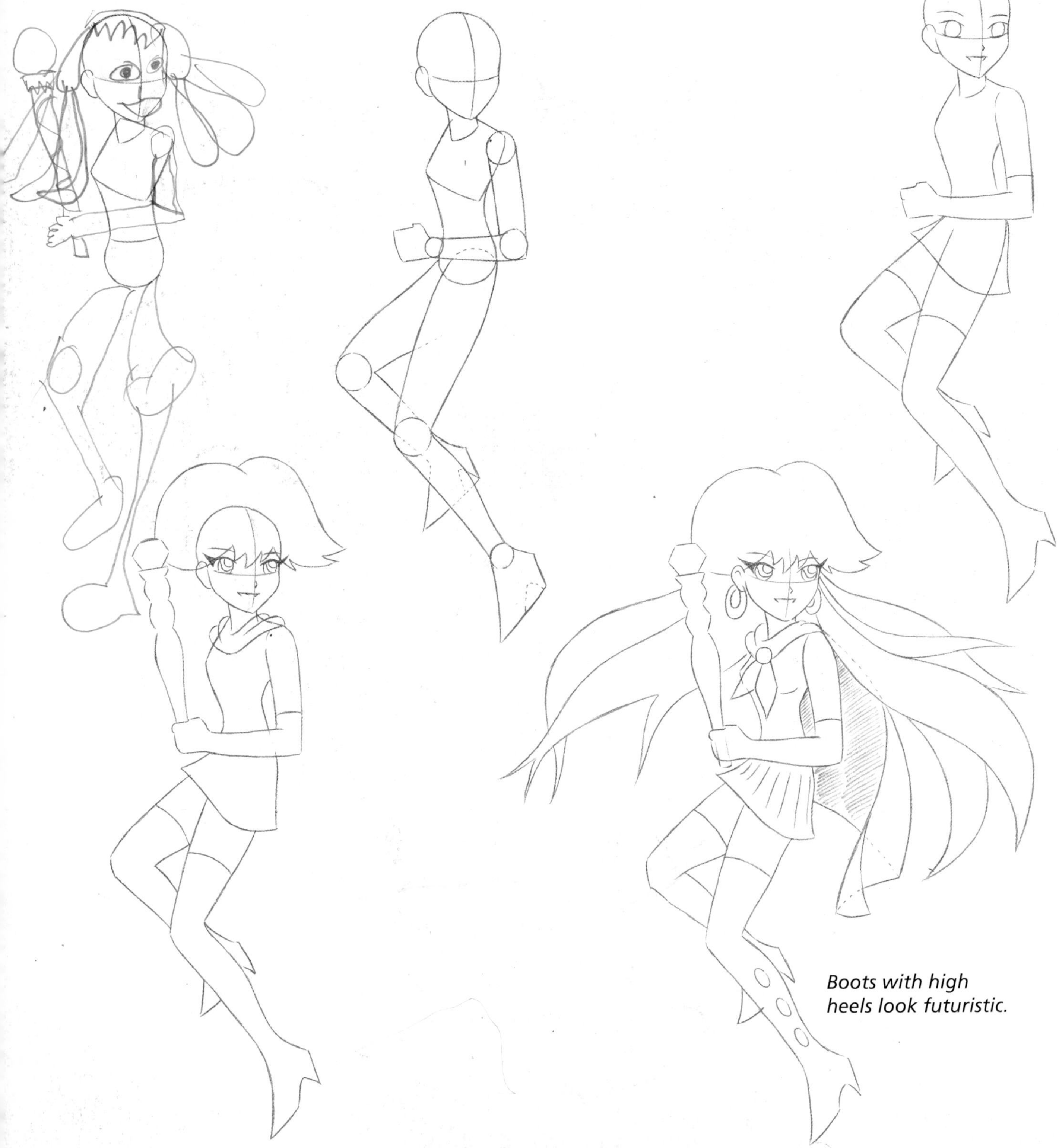

Boots with high heels look futuristic.

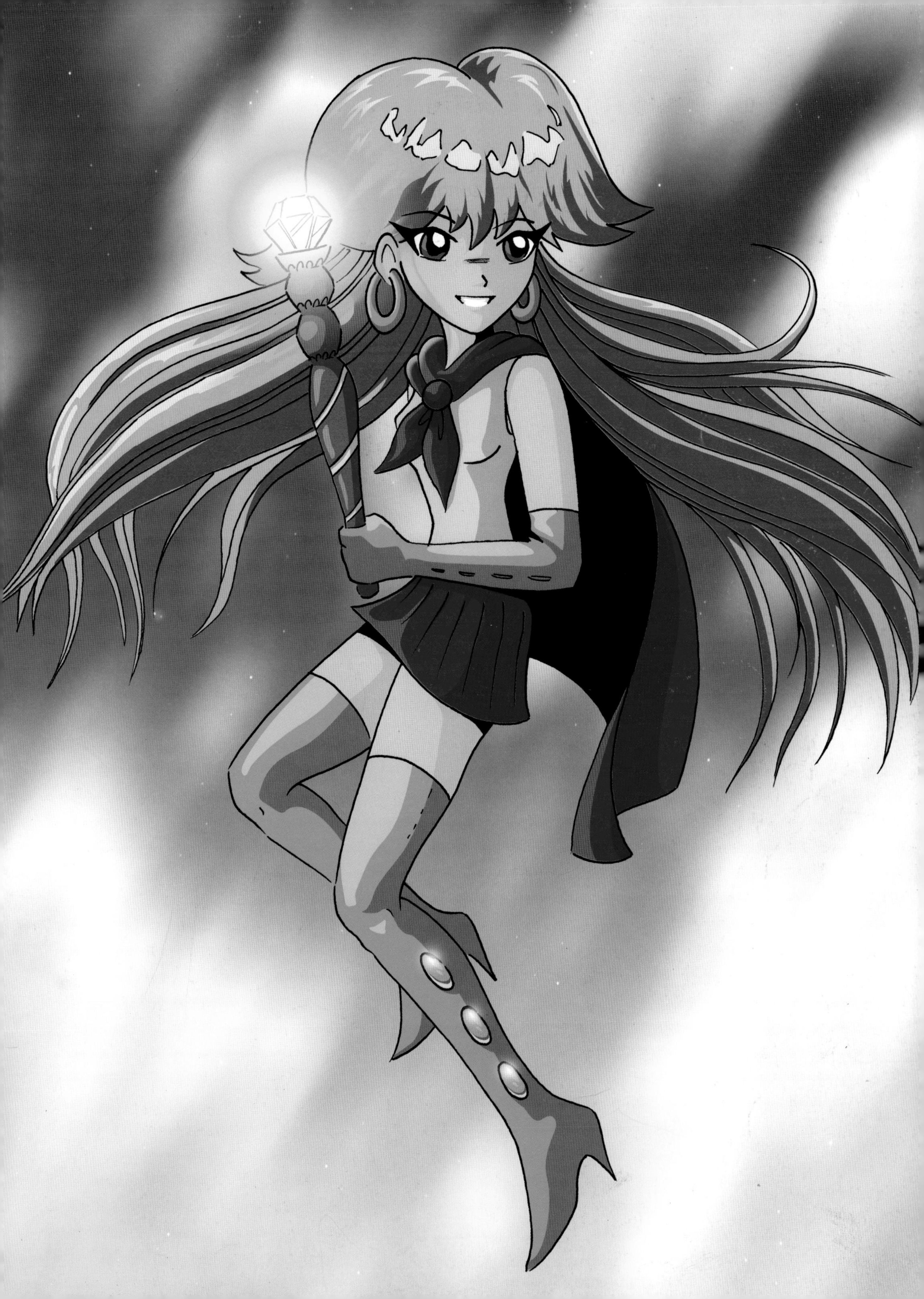

Fantasy Fighter

Sword in hand, the fantasy fighter is ready to take on the beasts of the netherworld! Note the long, flowing locks—and how about those cool swirls of hair on the sides of her head? Bracelets on the upper arm are used only for fantasy characters.

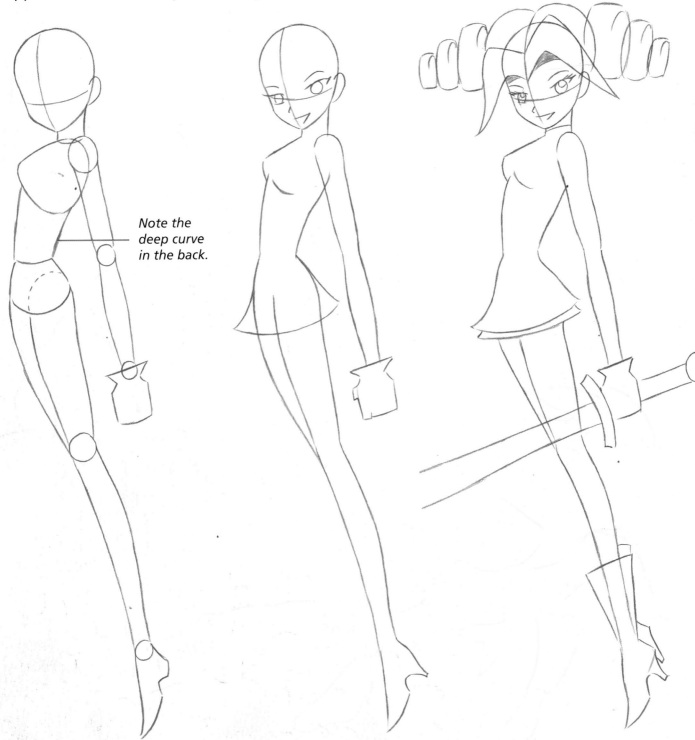

Note the deep curve in the back.

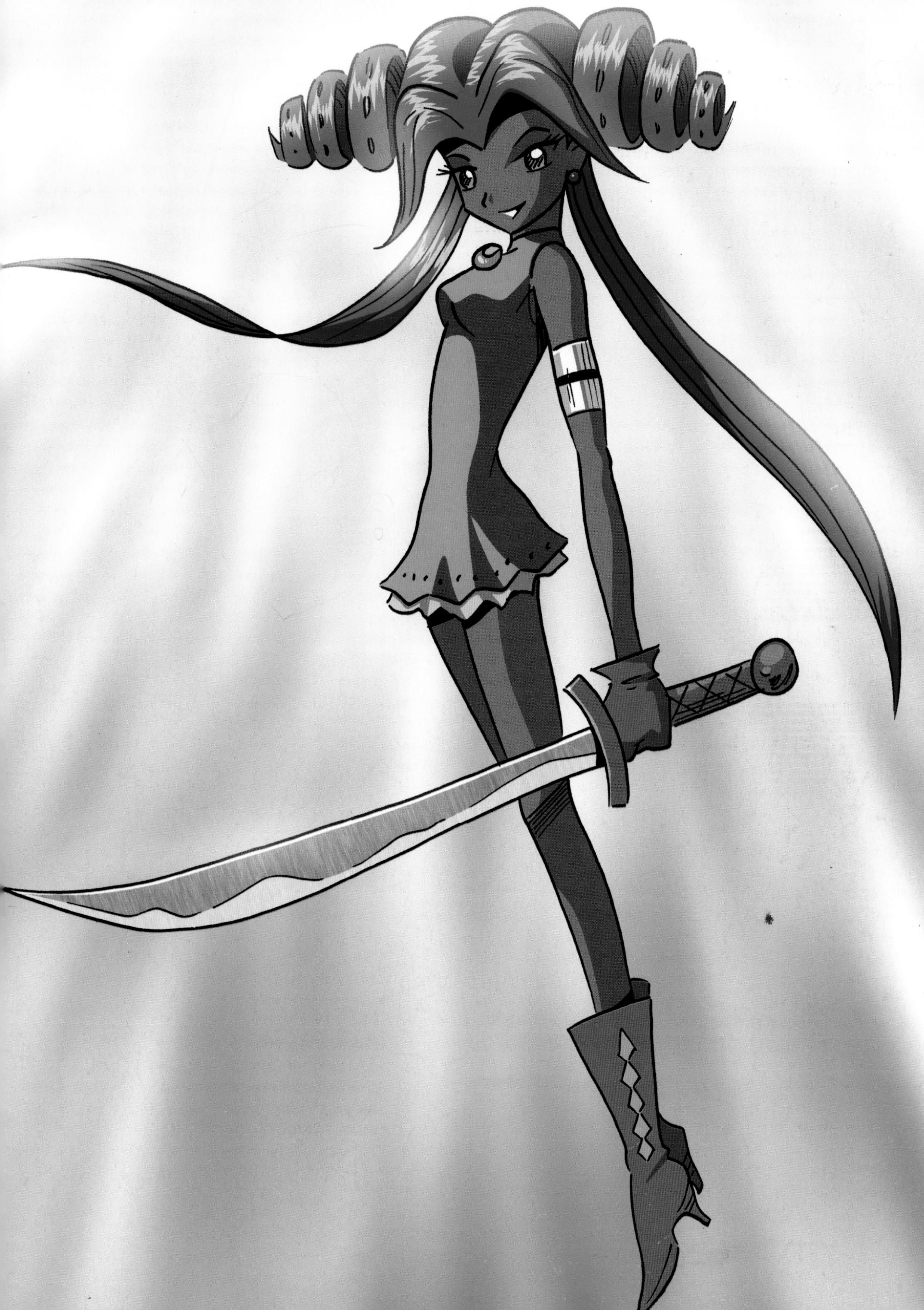

Hero Girl

This magical girl strikes a heroic pose as she defends her people against the lords of darkness and evil. Notice how she shows her enemies (yes, she's usually outnumbered!) that she is ready to fight. Her legs are in the classic flying position.

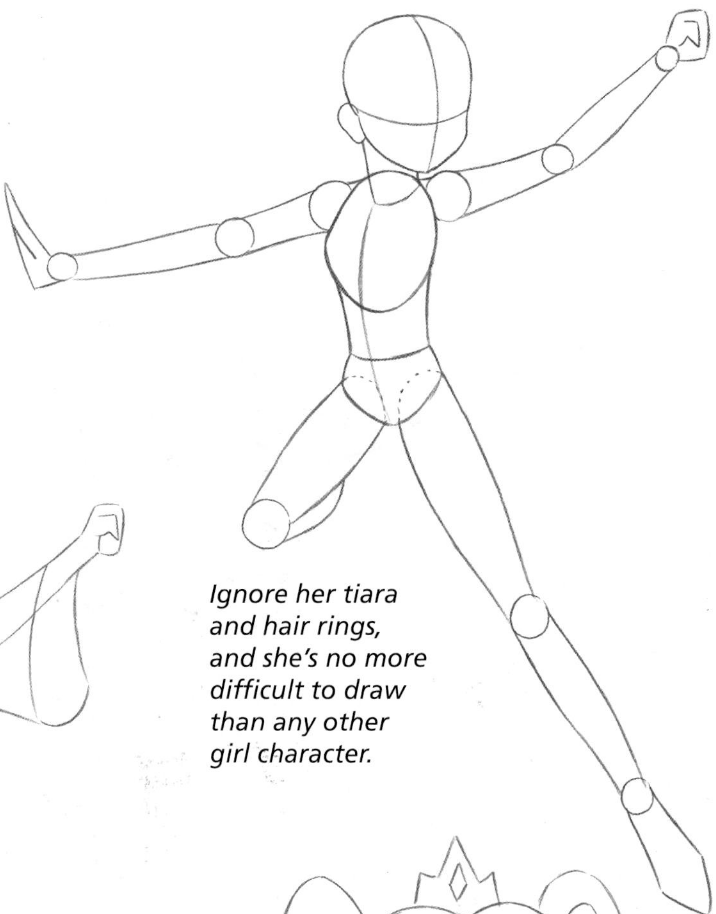

Ignore her tiara and hair rings, and she's no more difficult to draw than any other girl character.

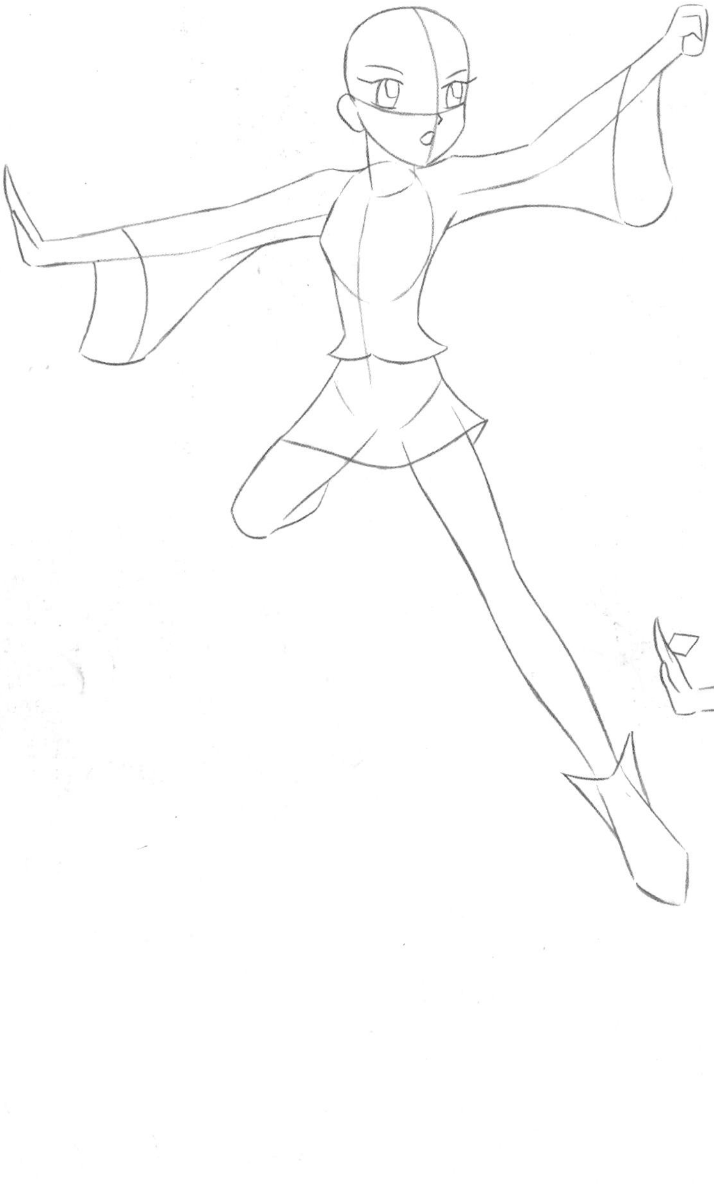

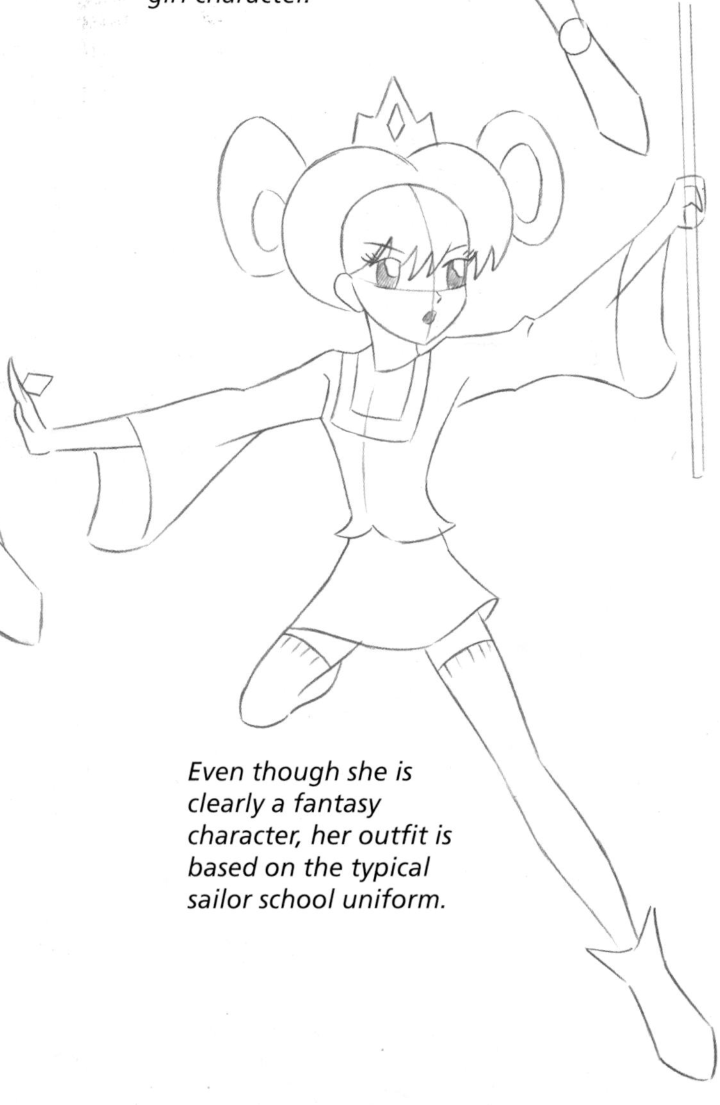

Even though she is clearly a fantasy character, her outfit is based on the typical sailor school uniform.

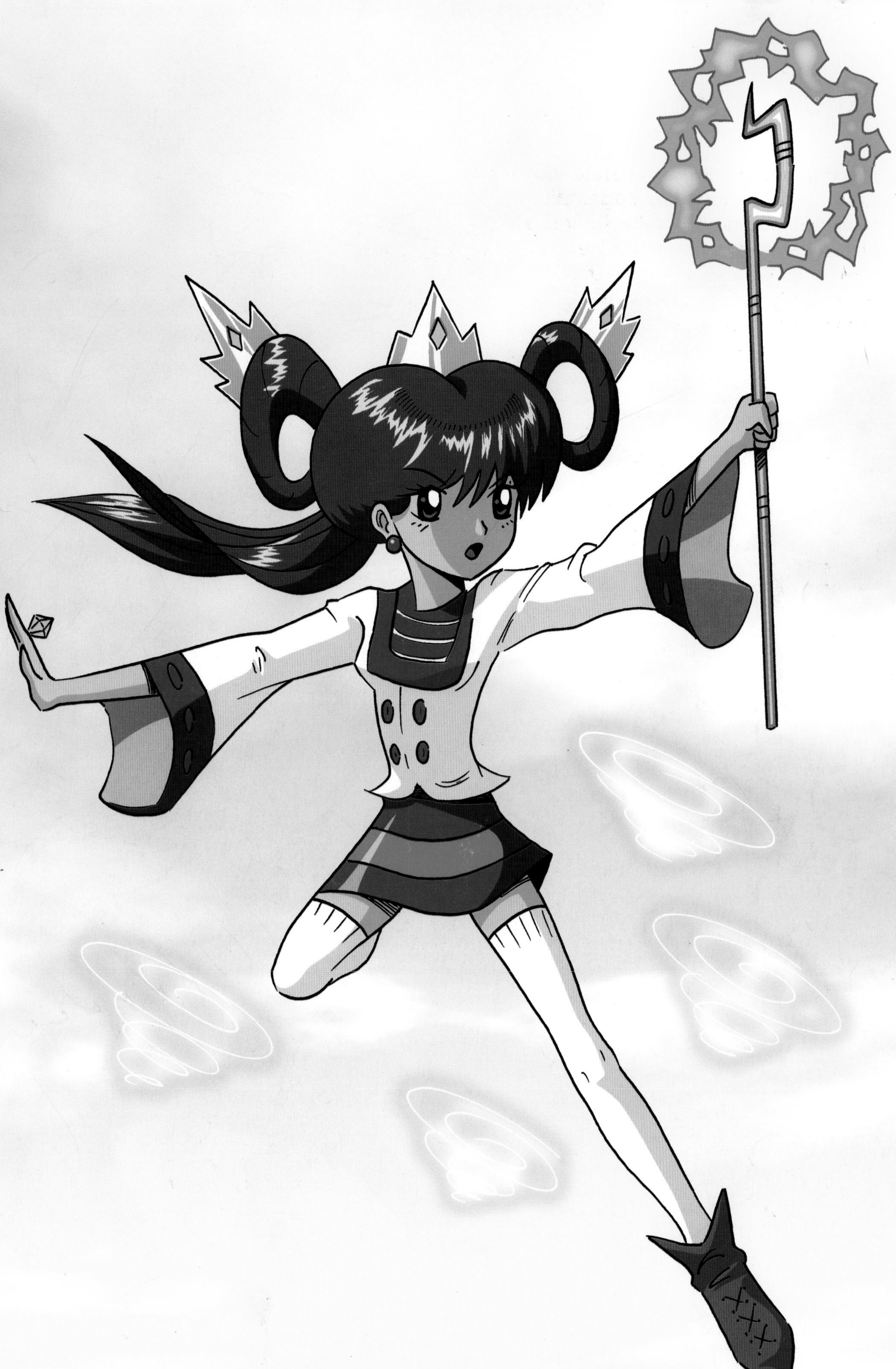

Magical Boy

Like the magical girl, the magical boy also puts on a souped-up costume to battle the bad guys. A cape with a high collar adds a dramatic touch.

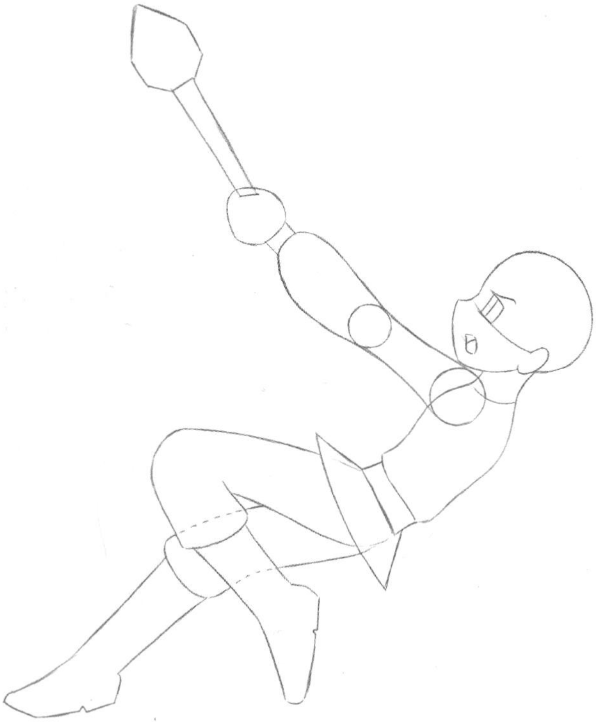

When objects overlap, "draw through" with very light lines to get the placement right.

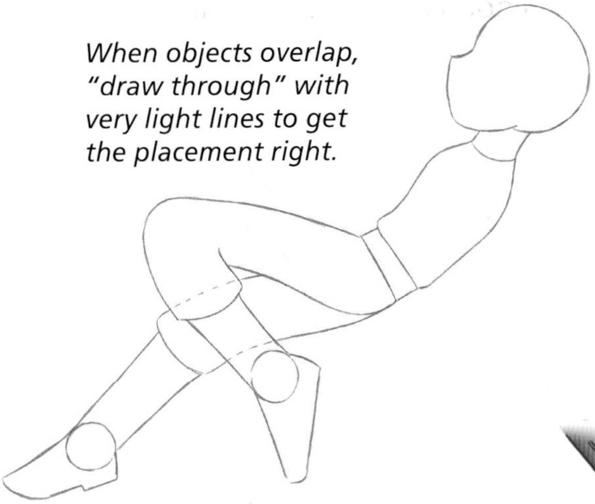

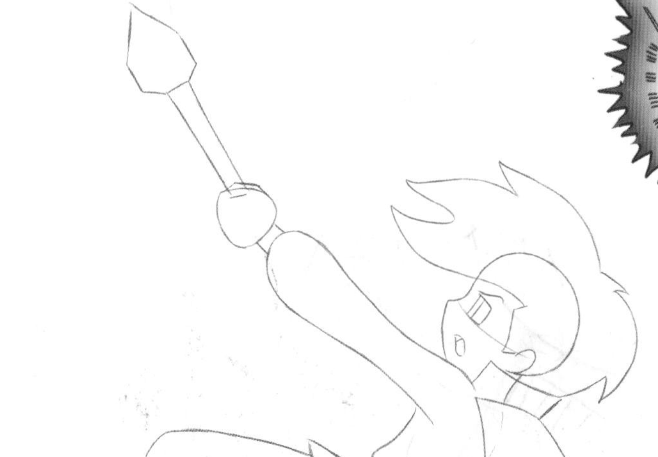

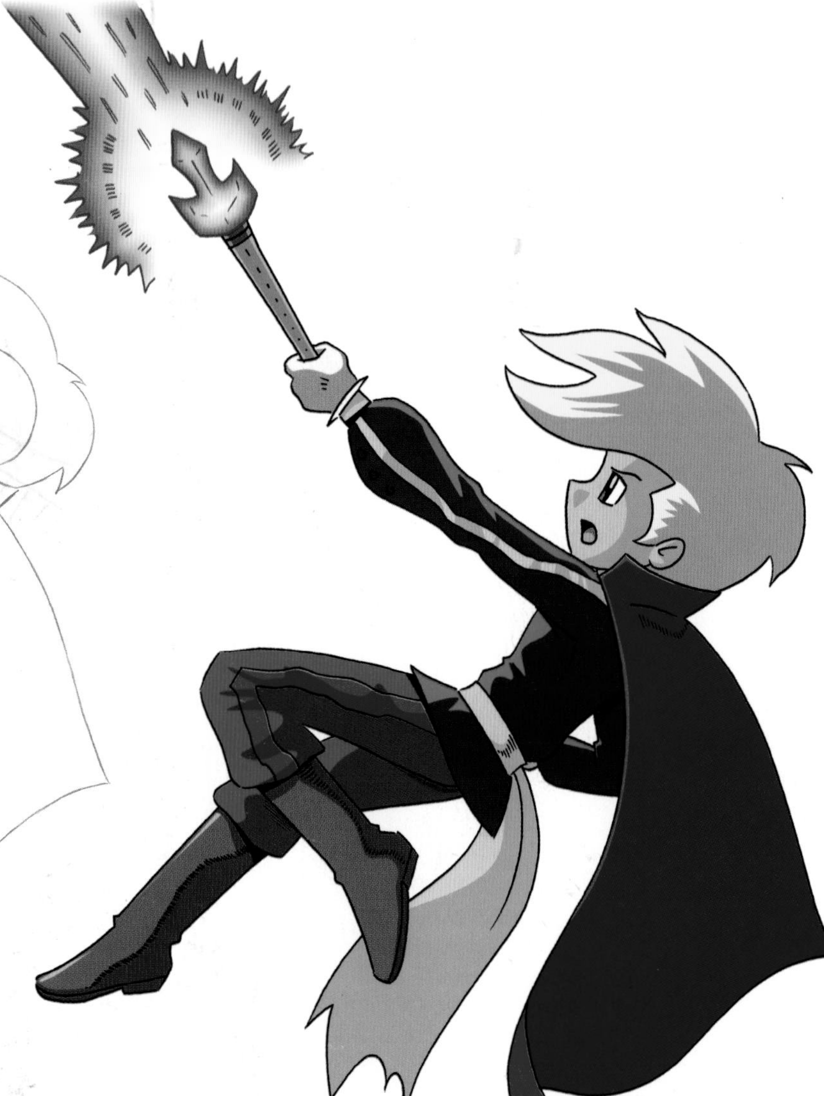

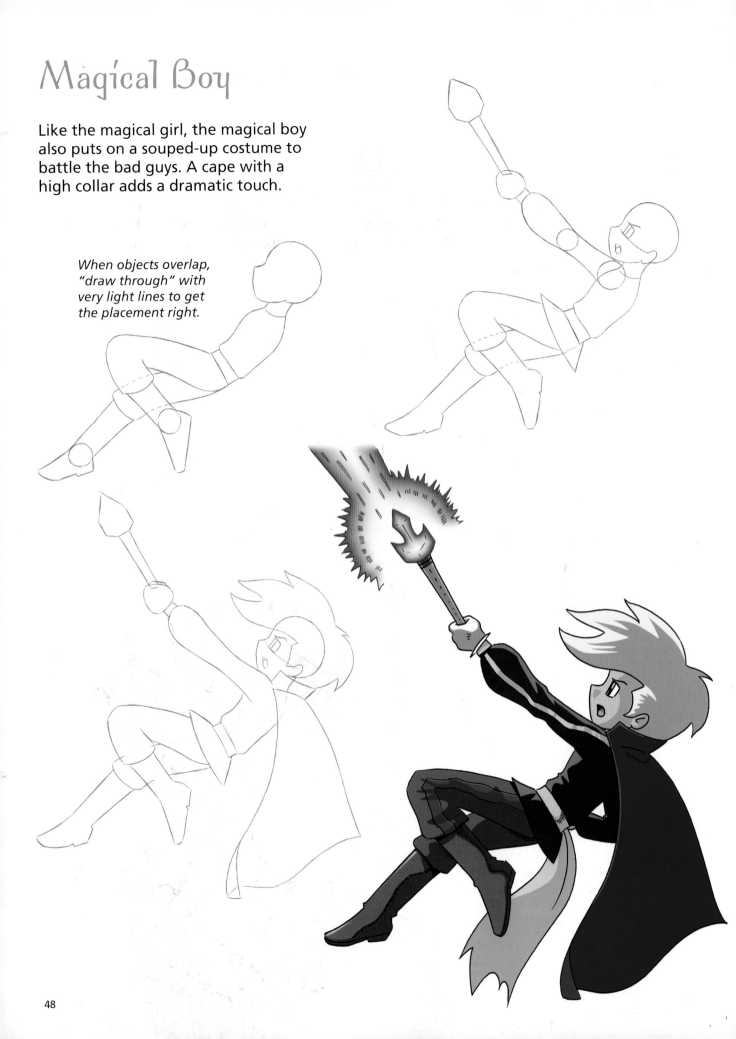

Planetary Commander

Intergalactic fighters appear all the time in shoujo. In science fiction, you'll often find two different ideas mixed together—for example, this character's uniform looks like something from the future; maybe it's the jacket of a soldier in a royal space force. Yet his weapon is low-tech: a simple sword. Combining the past with the future is a great way to create cool sci-fi manga characters.

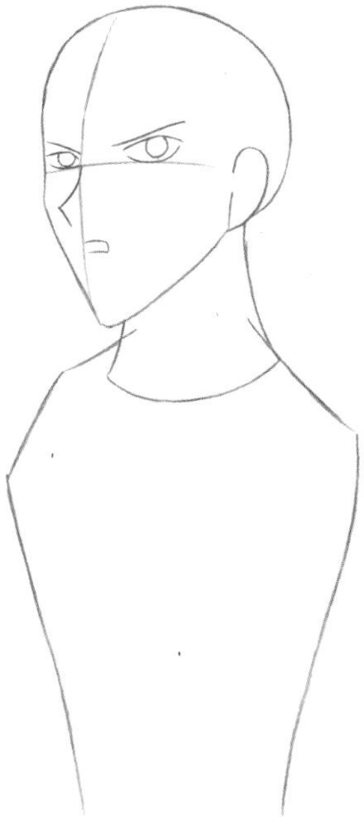

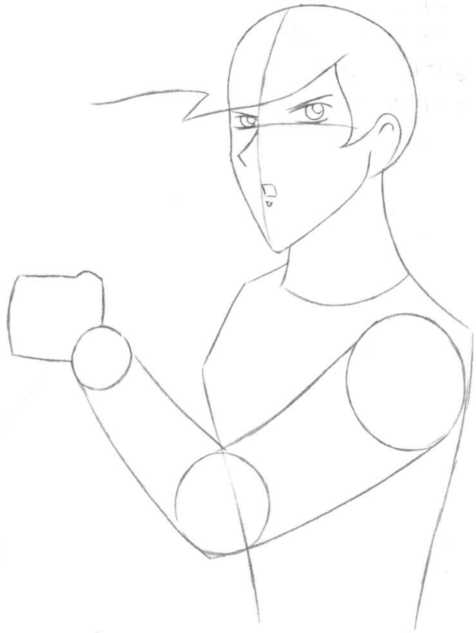

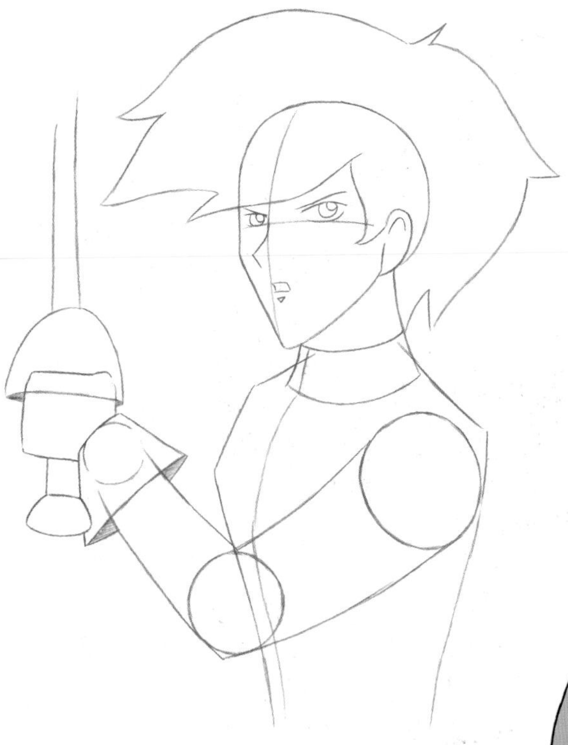

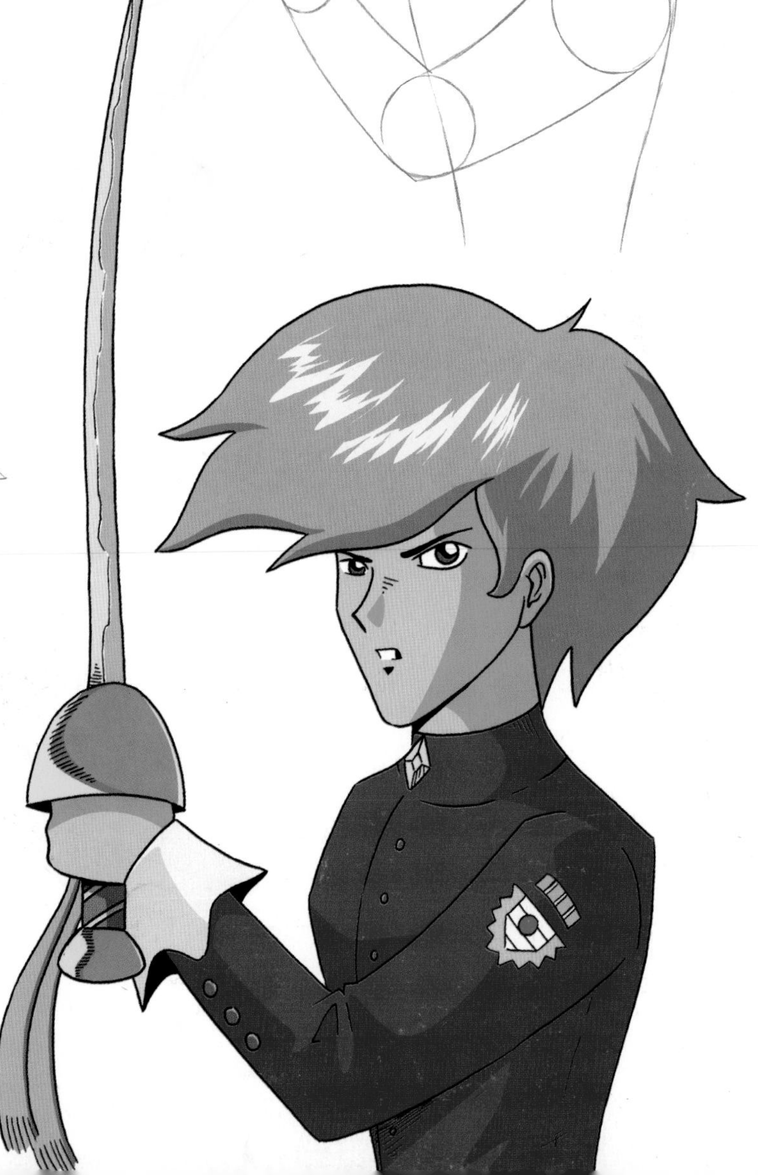

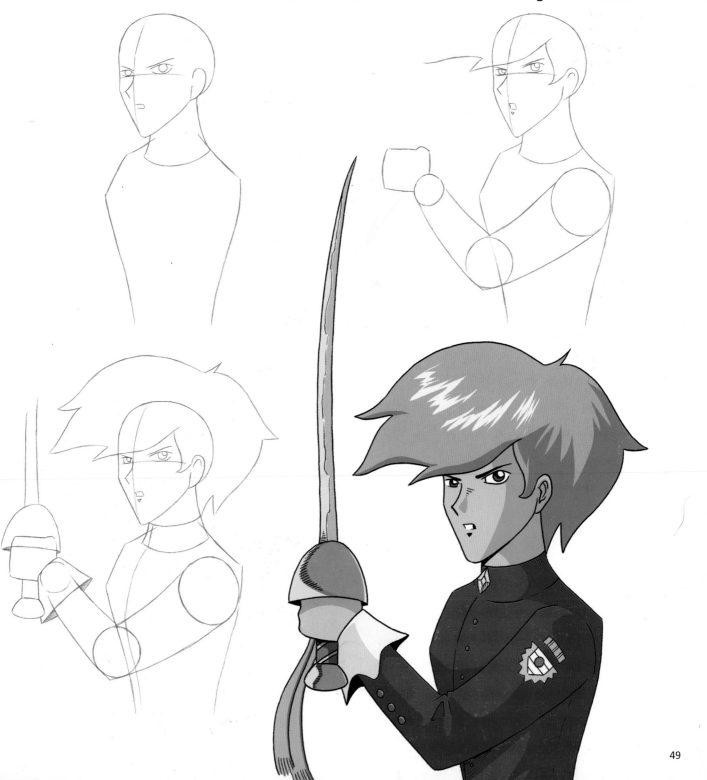

Boy with Special Powers

Boys with special powers fight on the same side as magical girls. These boys don't have to change costumes, the way the magical girls and boys do. They often have mystical weapons. But don't let the magic sword do all the work for you! You still need to draw a good pose. A cool martial arts stance works well for fight scenes.

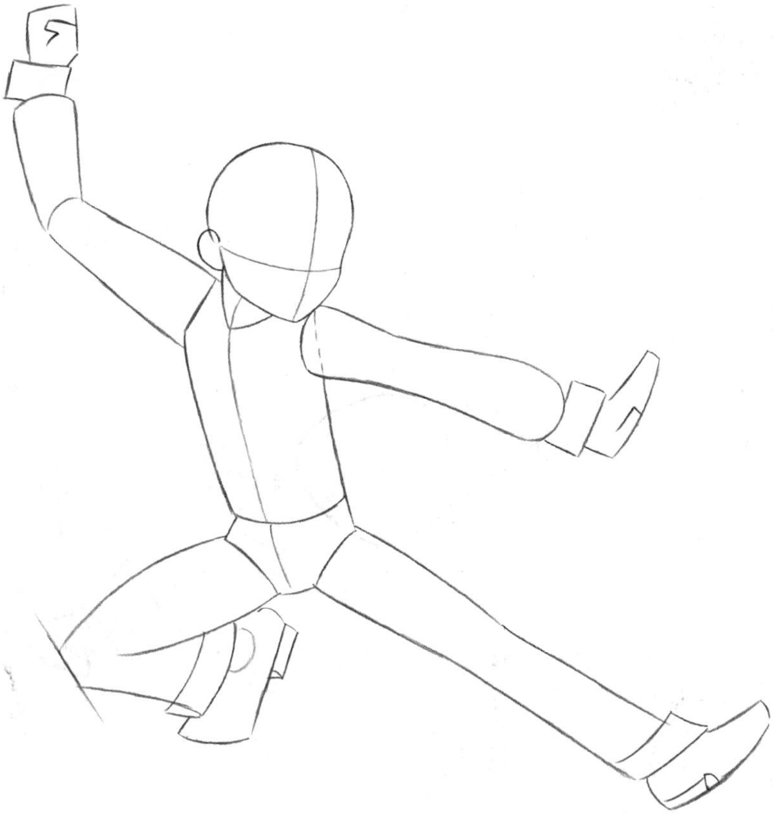

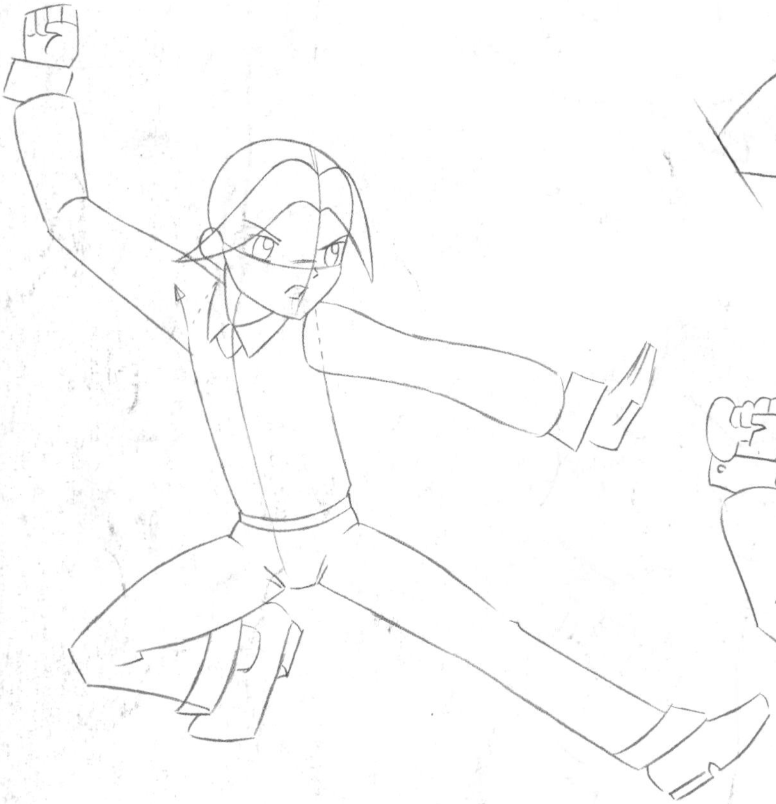

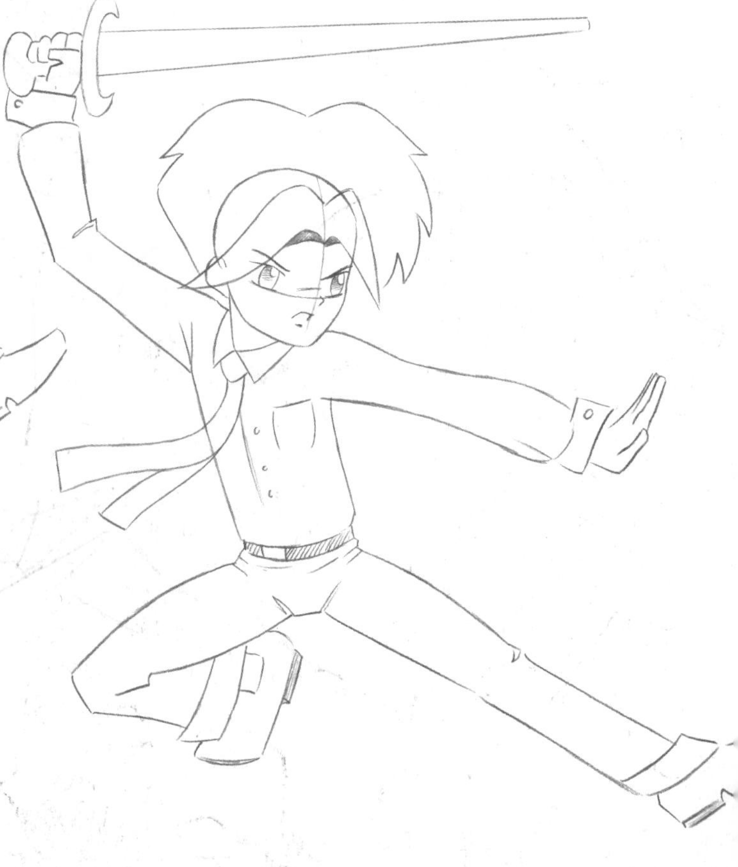

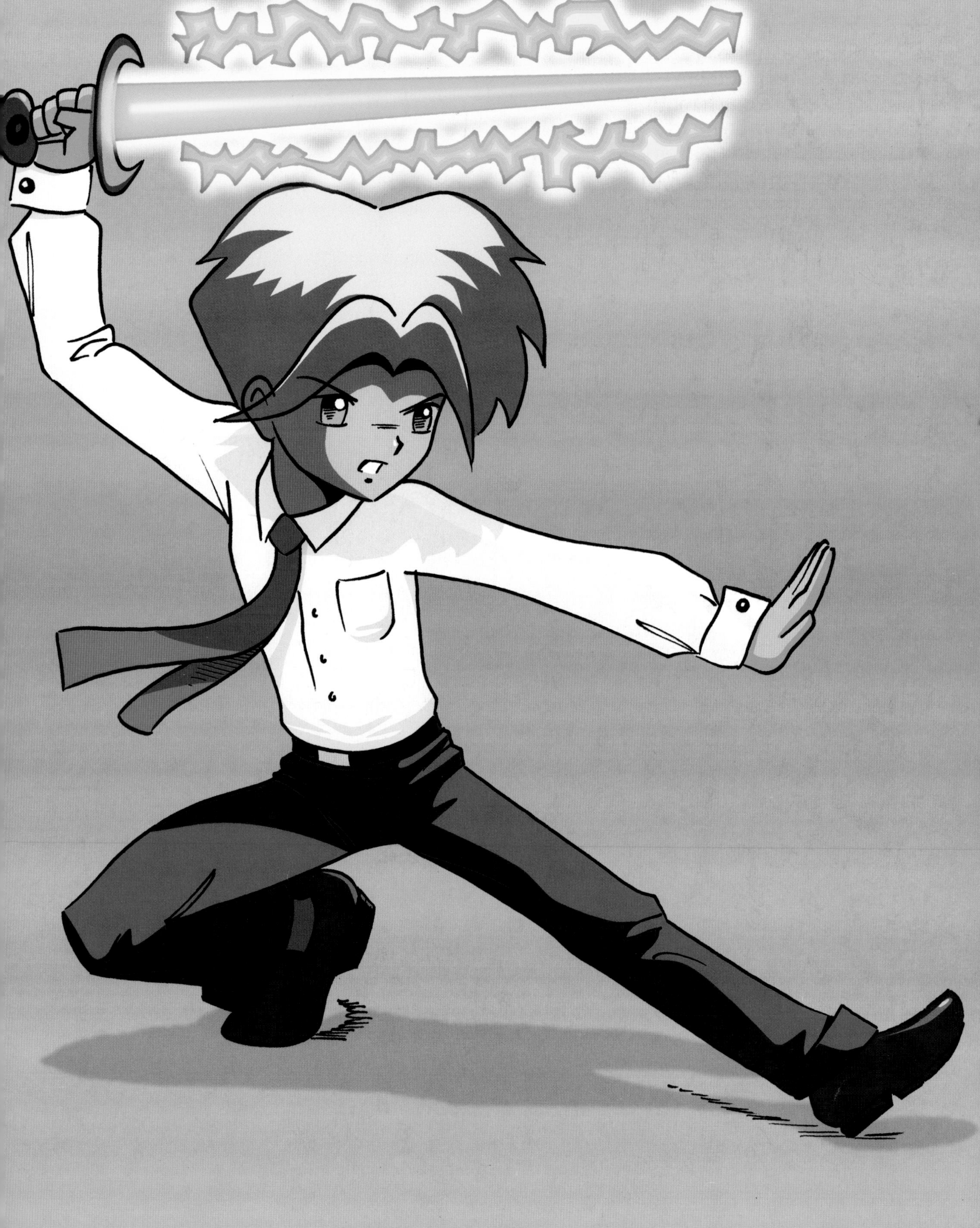

Gallant Knight

Bishies make great medieval heroes. But don't put them in armor. They are much more dramatic when costumed in wide-collar shirts with puffed-out sleeves, a sash at the waist, and high boots.

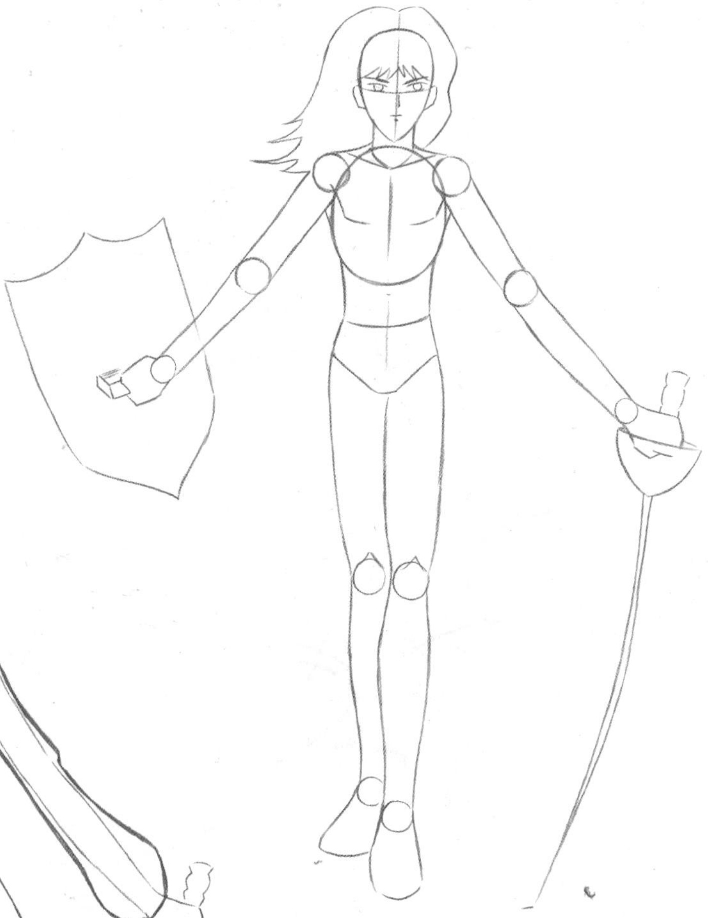

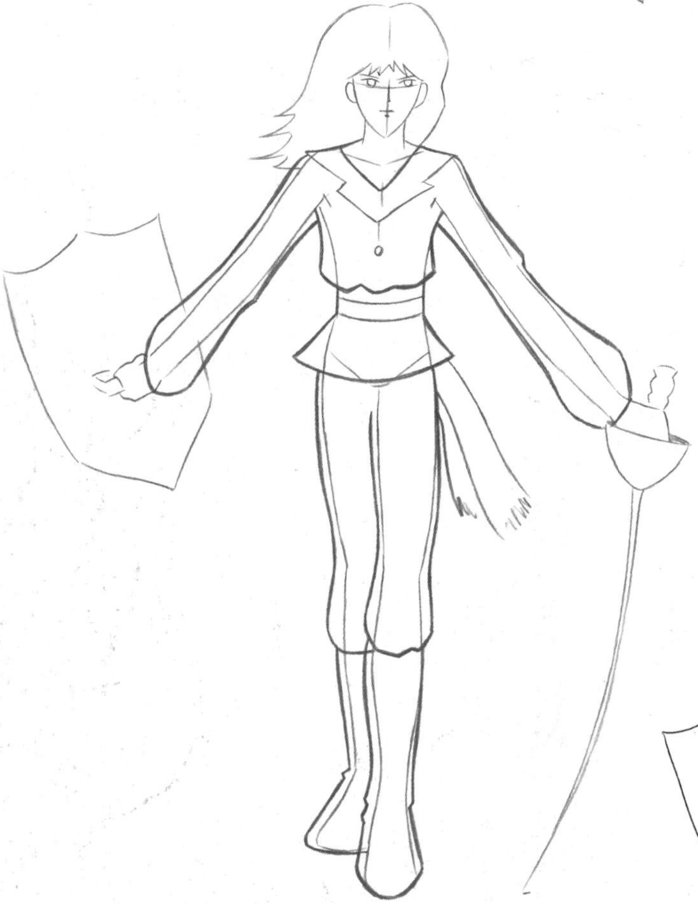

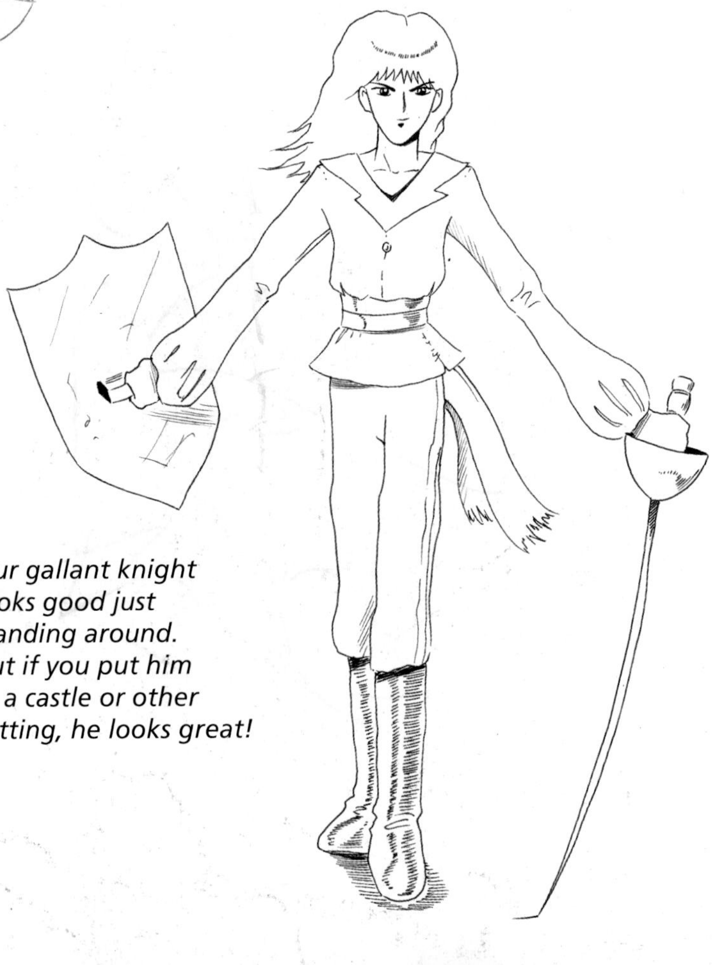

Our gallant knight looks good just standing around. But if you put him in a castle or other setting, he looks great!

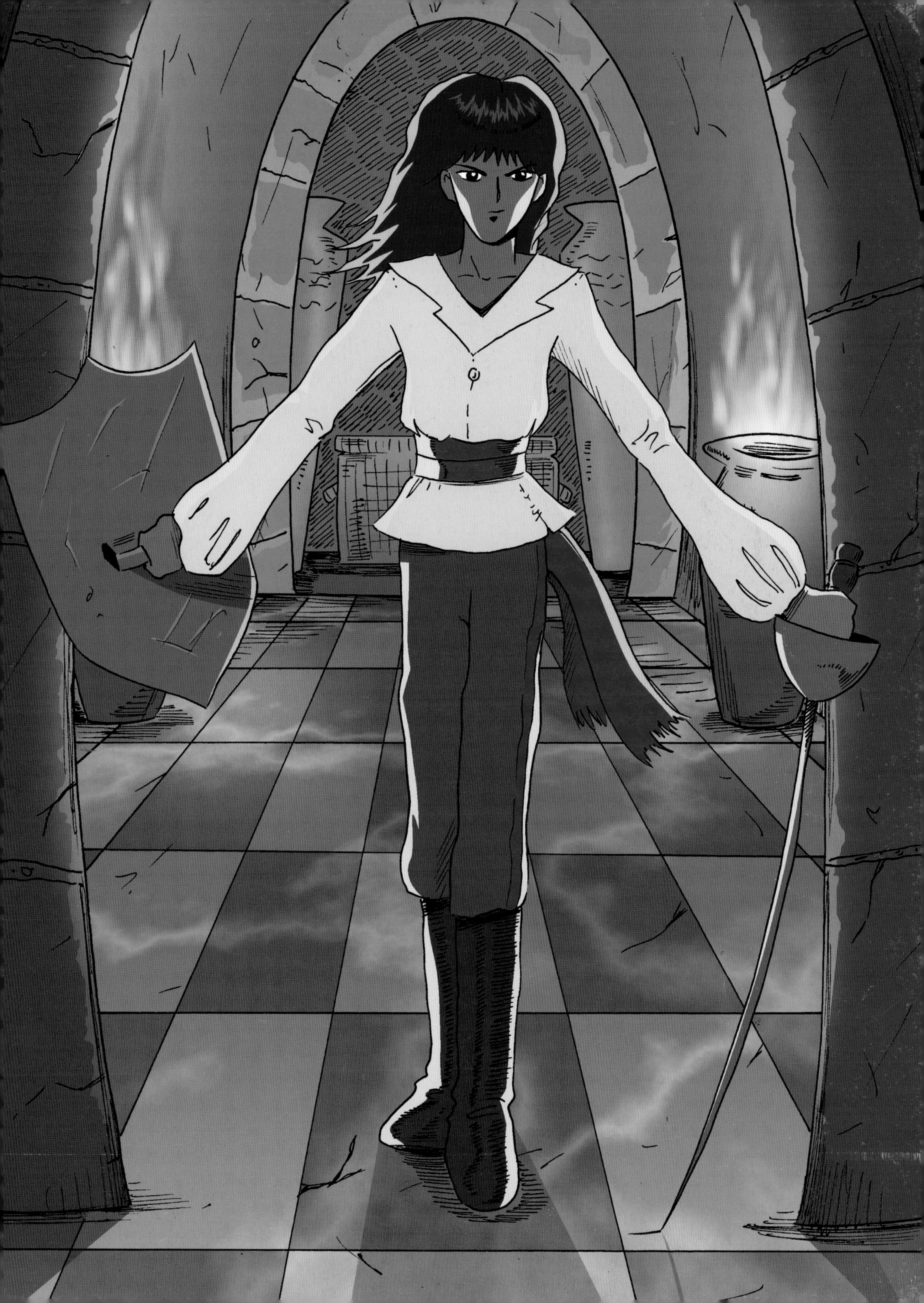

Demigod

Demigods and their female counterparts, goddesses, are very appealing. Ethereal beings, they can appear and disappear at will. They use their tremendous power wisely, and they are always drawn as if they are floating above the ground.

SIMPLIFYING FOLDS

To draw a flowing hem on a robe, just follow these three steps.

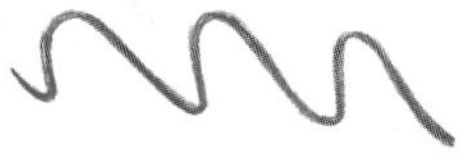

1. First, draw a squiggly line with hills and valleys.

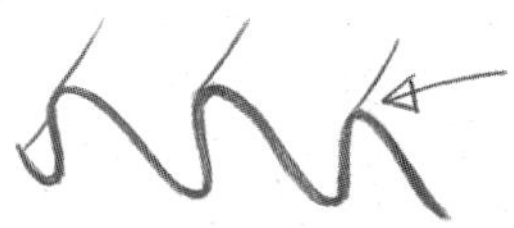

2. Connect lines to the tops of the hills.

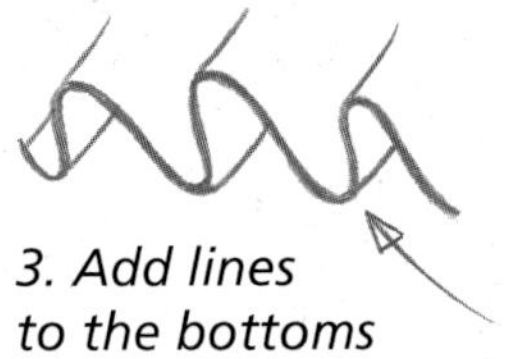

3. Add lines to the bottoms of the valleys.

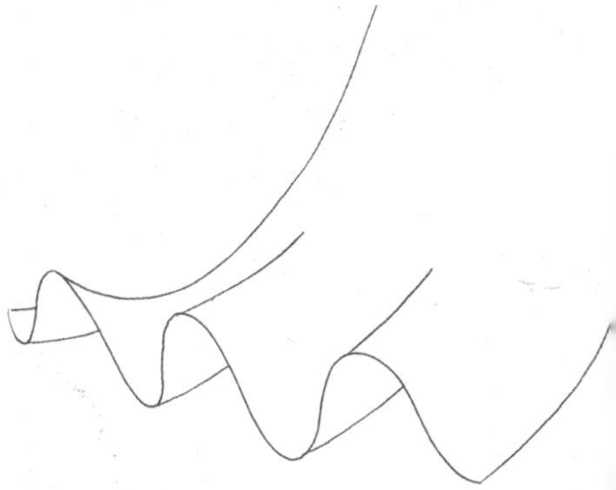

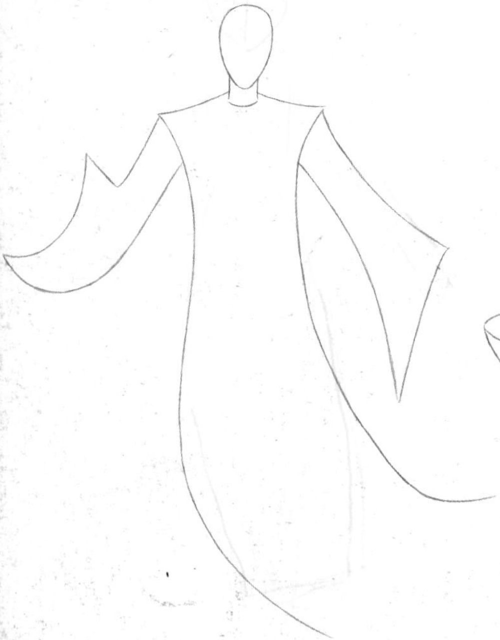

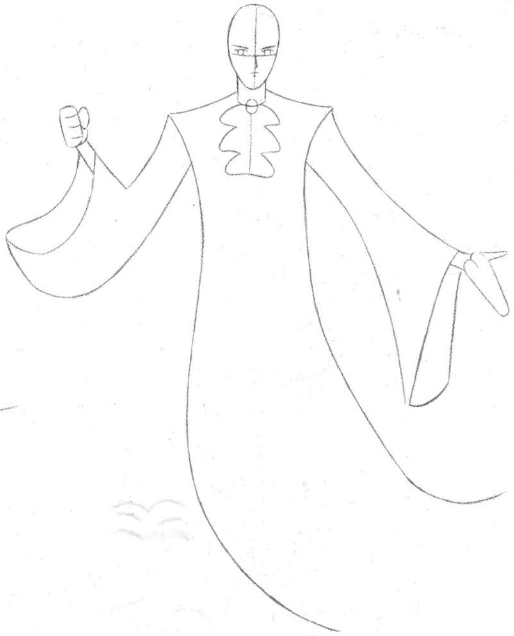

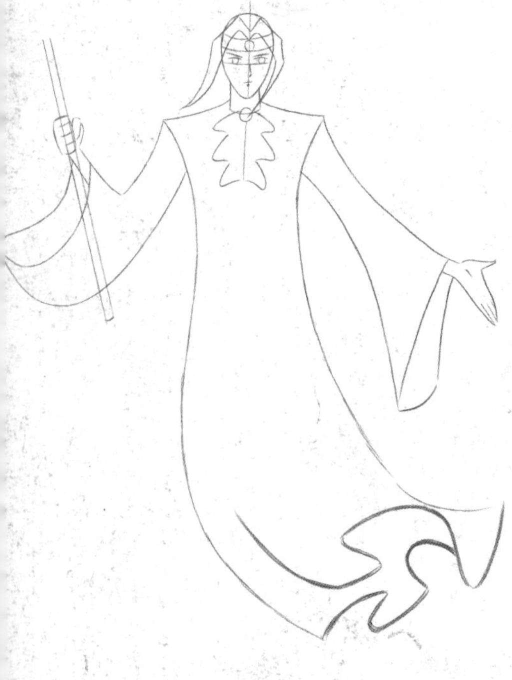

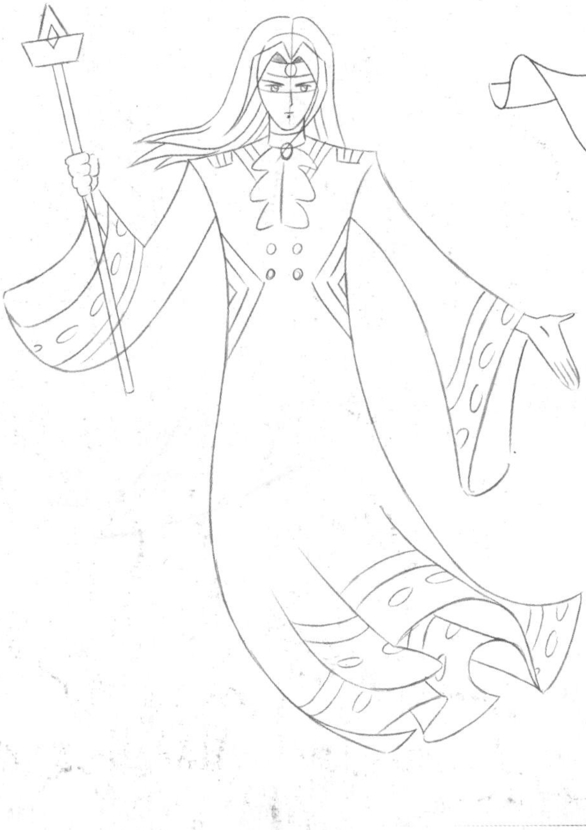

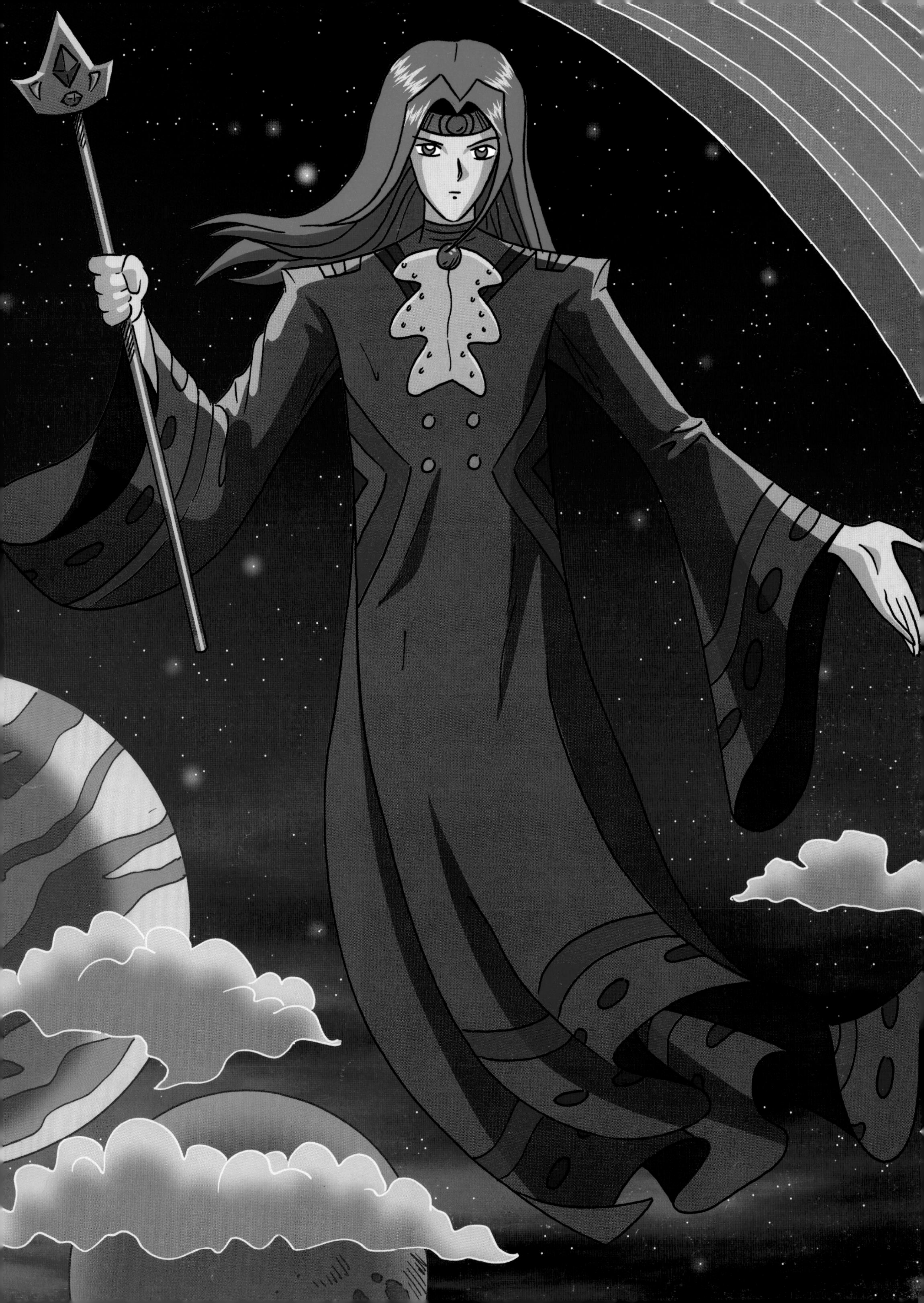

Goddess

To make a goddess, all you have to do is draw a pretty woman, make the hair and the dress longer, and add wings.

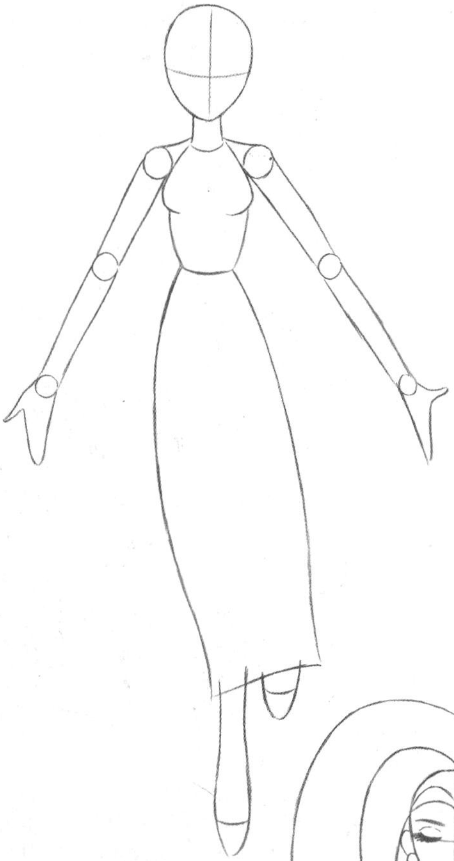

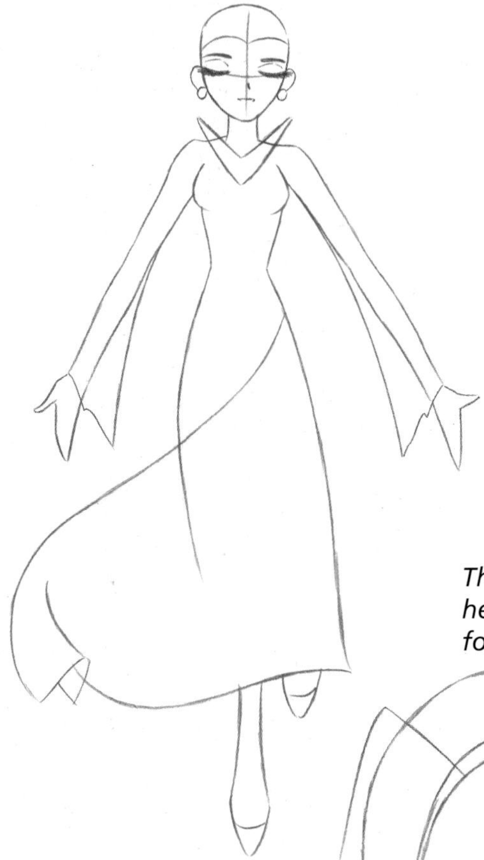

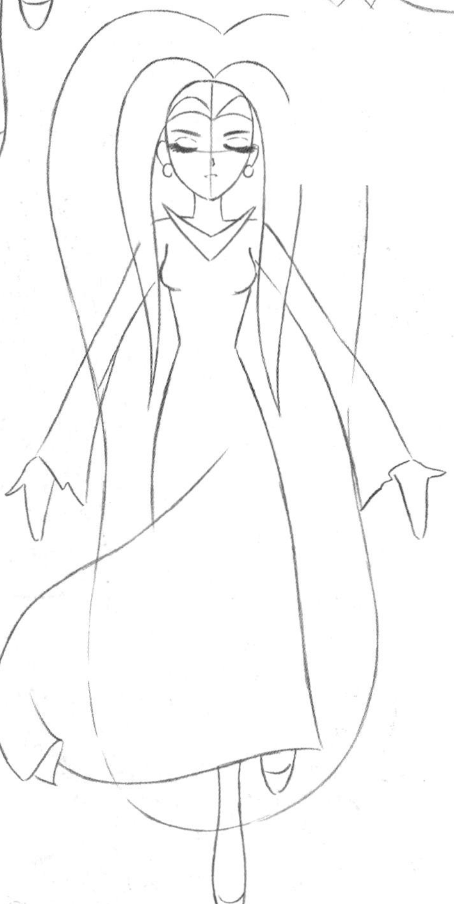

The ponytail on top of the head is always a good look for goddess characters.

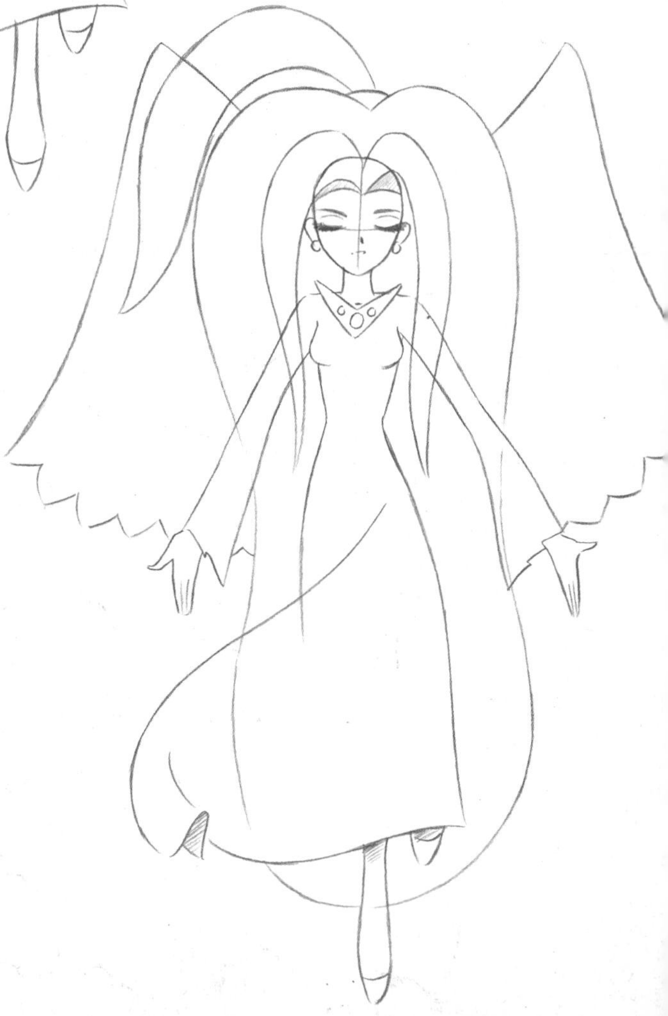

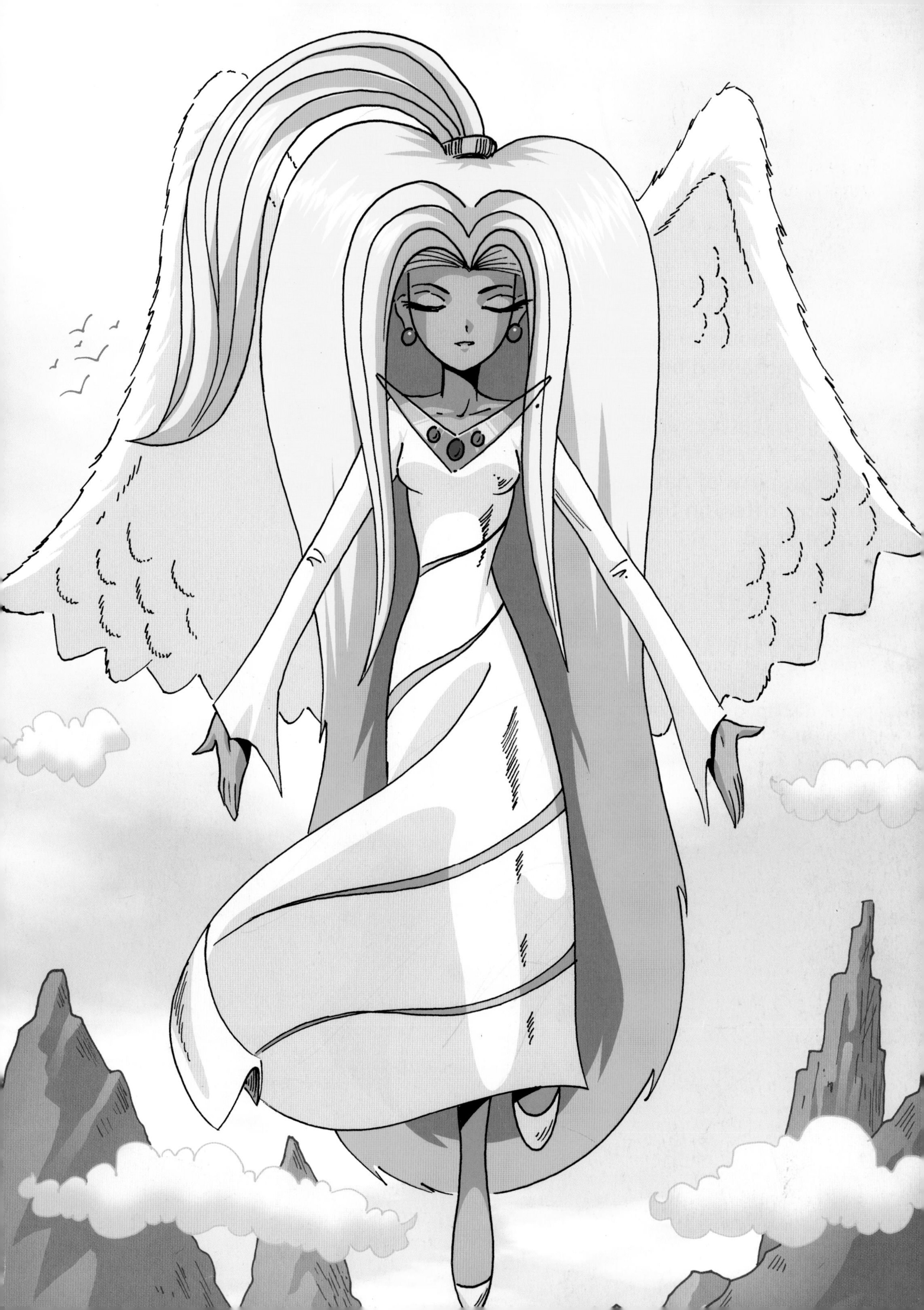

FAIRIES AND FRIENDS

Some of the best-loved characters of shoujo are the enchanted beings, with their delicate, beautiful features and expressive eyes. These magical spirits of nature are most often on the side of good.

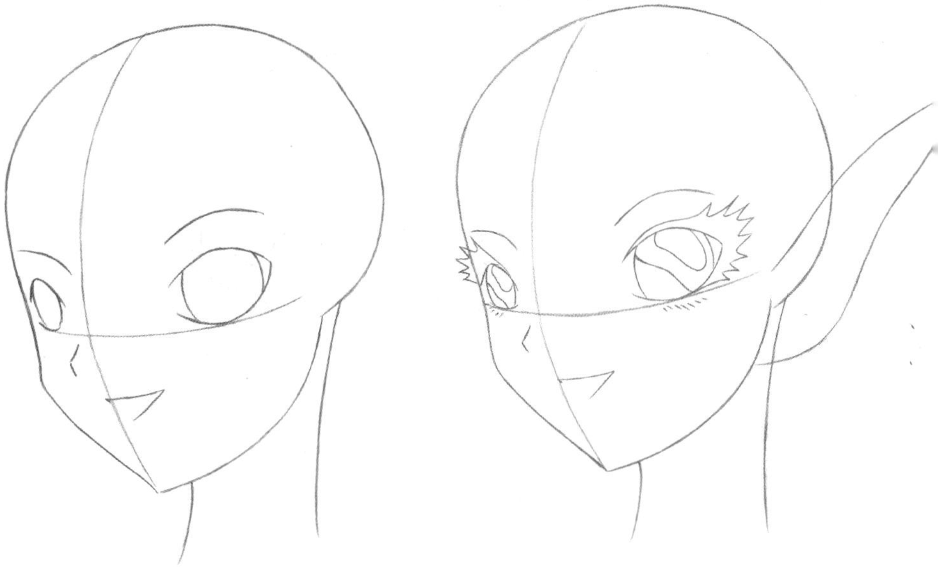

Fairy Girl

Young fairies have wide faces with very large eyes that show innocence and honesty. The almond-shaped eyes should be tilted up at the ends.

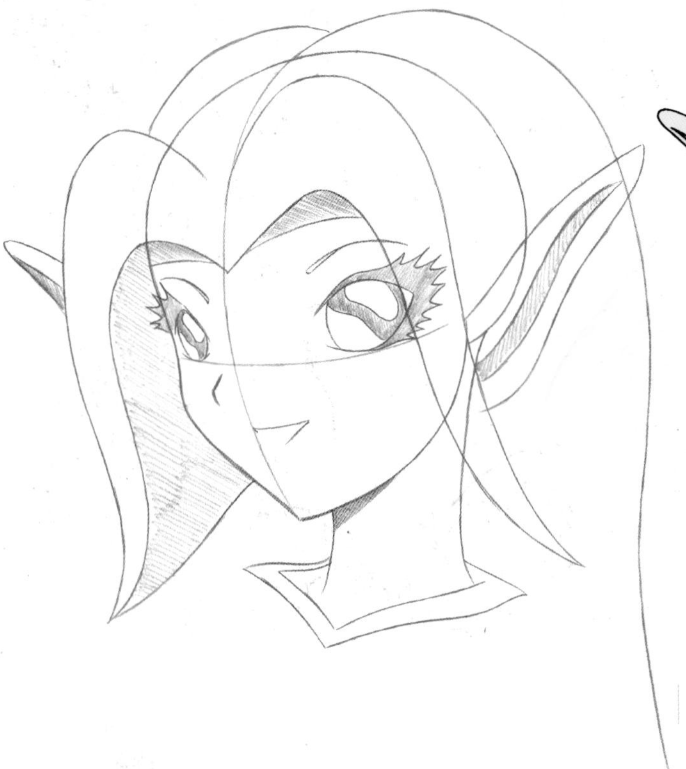

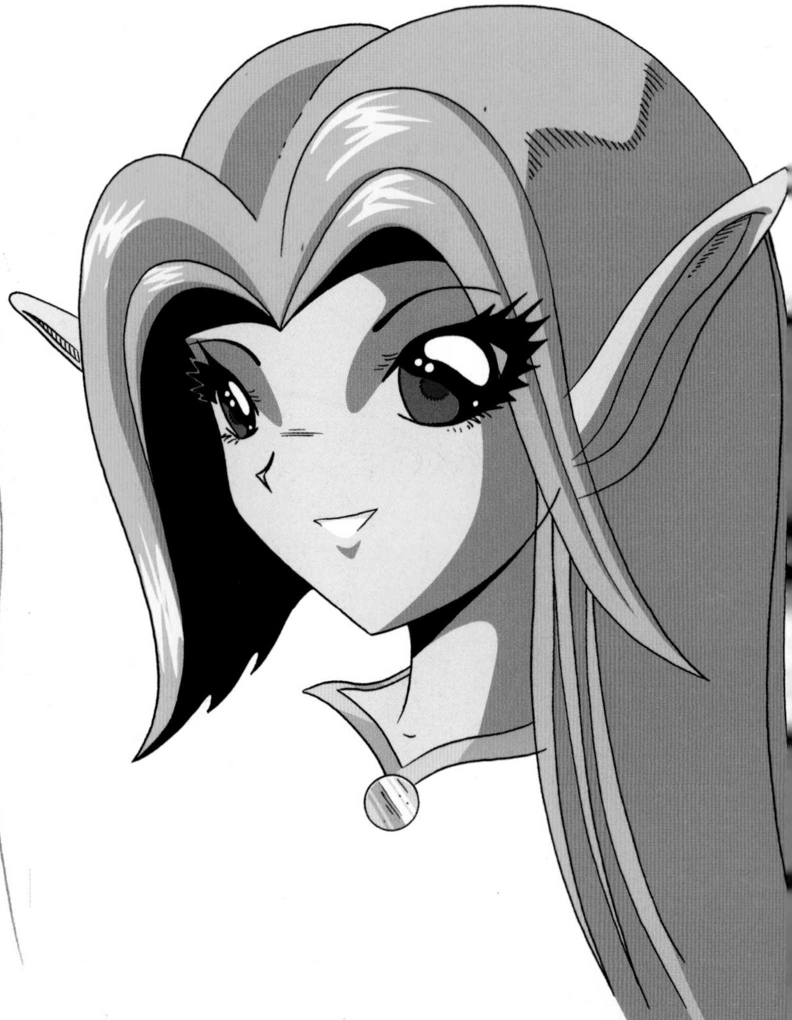

Fantasy Princess

Princesses are always pretty, and this character is no exception. The cone-shaped headpieces on either side of her head resemble the buns that were worn by the upper classes in the Middle Ages. The tiara shows that she is of noble birth.

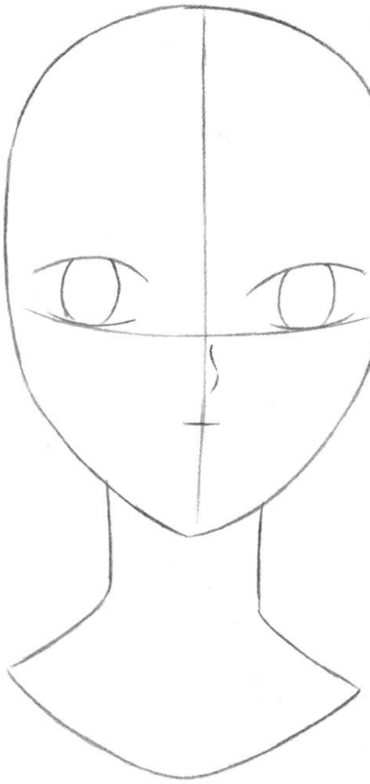

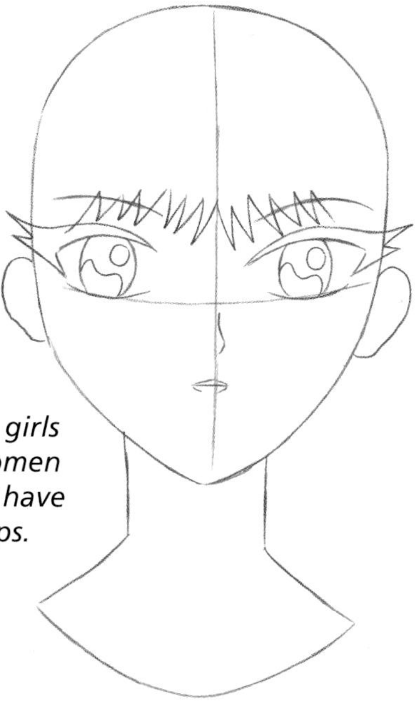

Manga girls and women usually have small lips.

Tiaras are small and delicate.

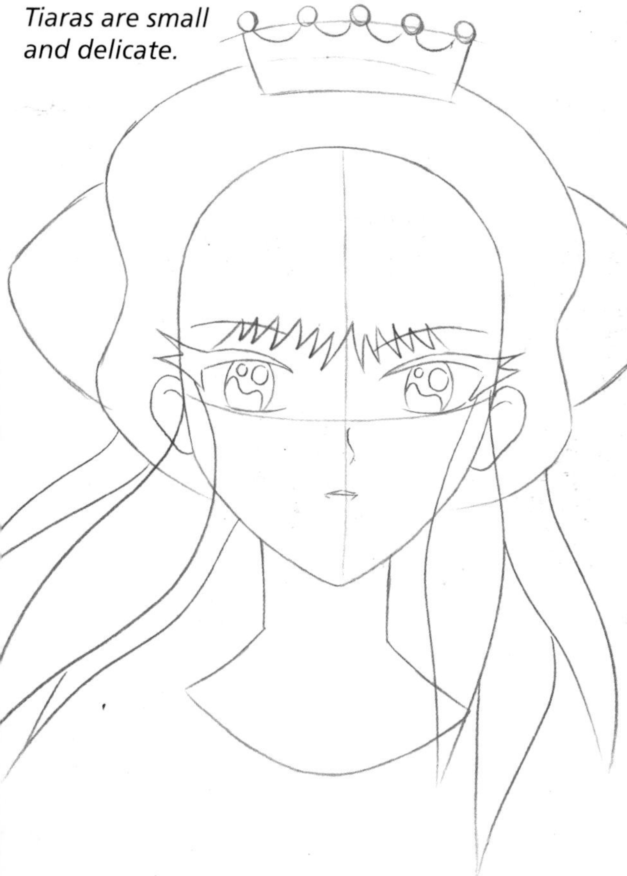

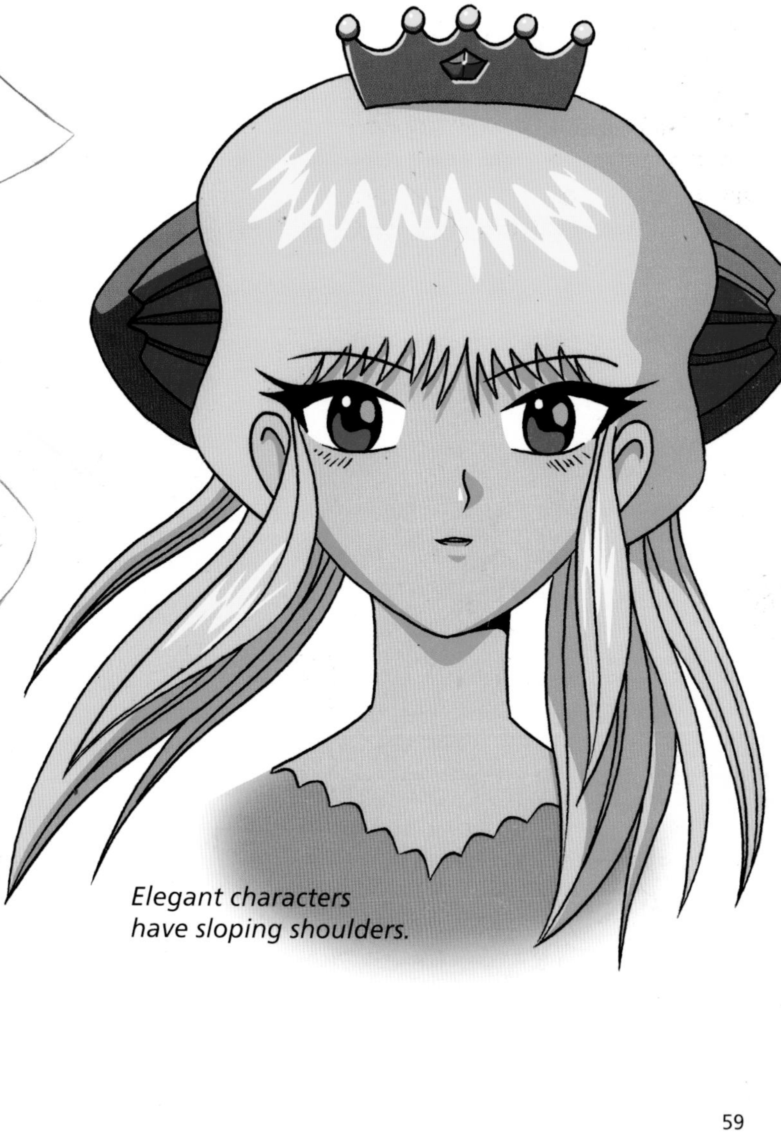

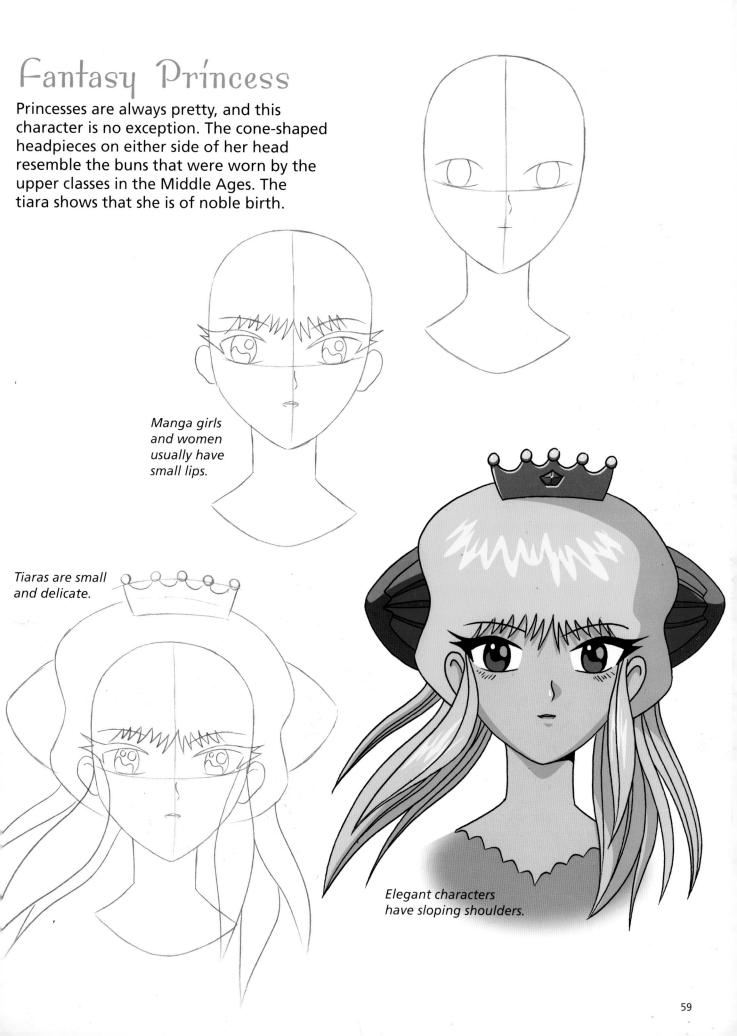

Elegant characters have sloping shoulders.

Elfin Queen

The fancy cones, jeweled choker, and long, flowing hair give this elfin queen a graceful quality, as do her beautiful eyes. The ears are very long, in the shoujo style of fairies and elves.

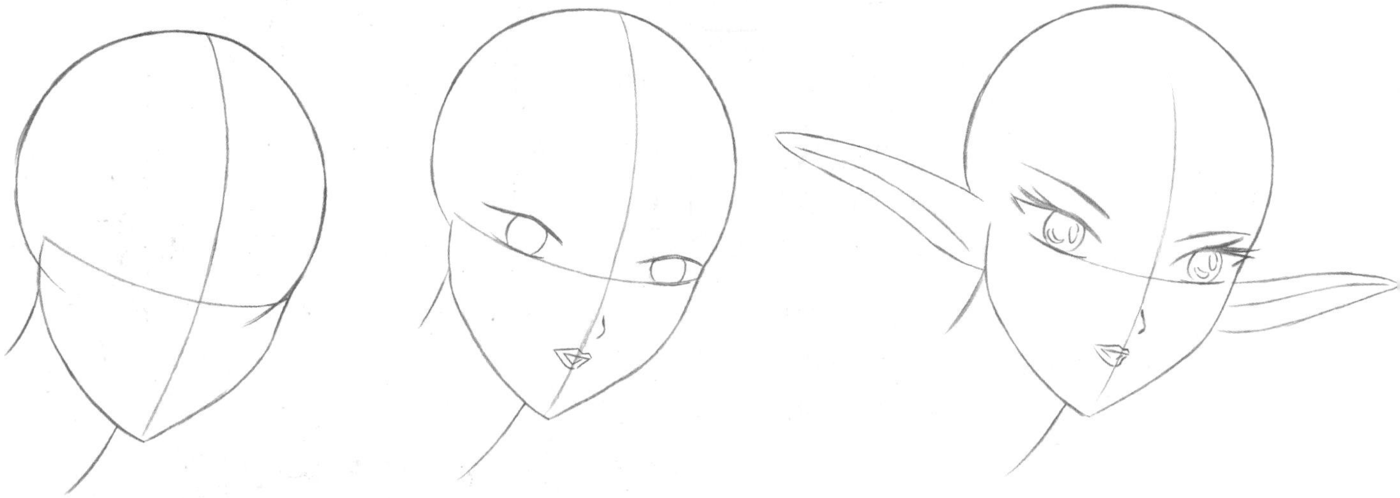

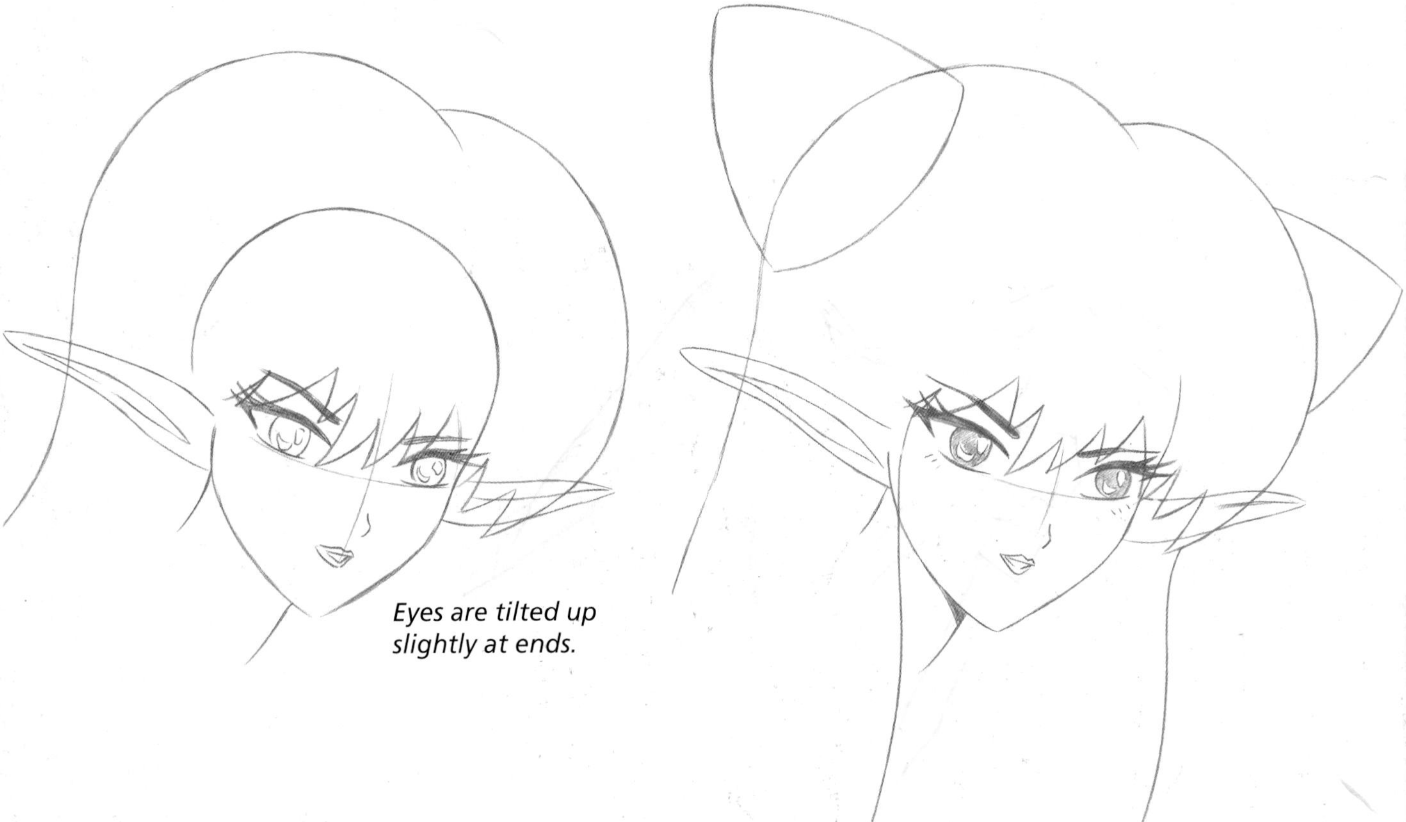
Eyes are tilted up slightly at ends.

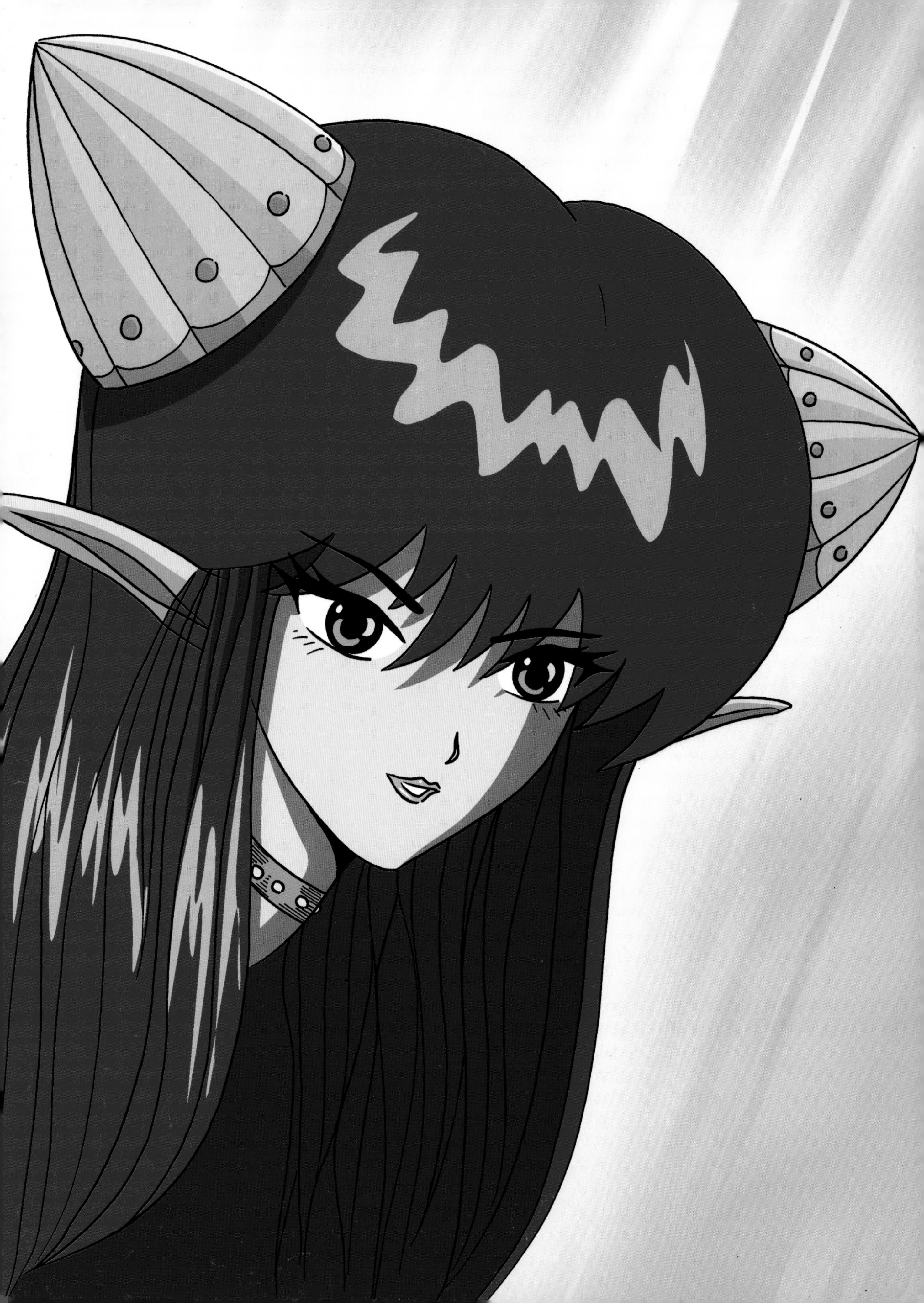

Flying Fairy

Fairies are creatures of earth and nature, and so their clothing should look natural—nothing too fancy. In fact, fairies can even go barefoot. Fairy wings are not drawn with feathers, but like the wings of a bee.

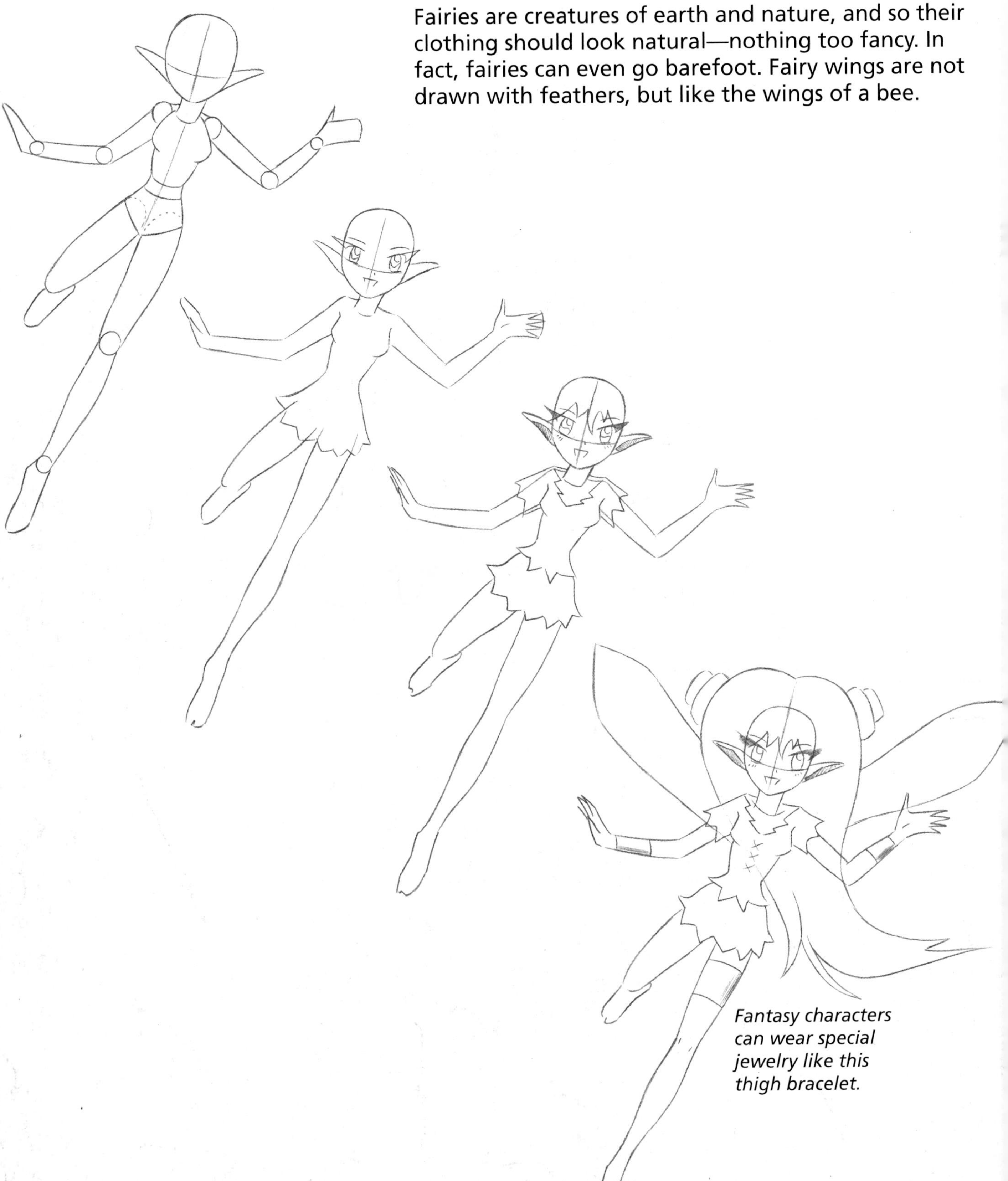

Fantasy characters can wear special jewelry like this thigh bracelet.

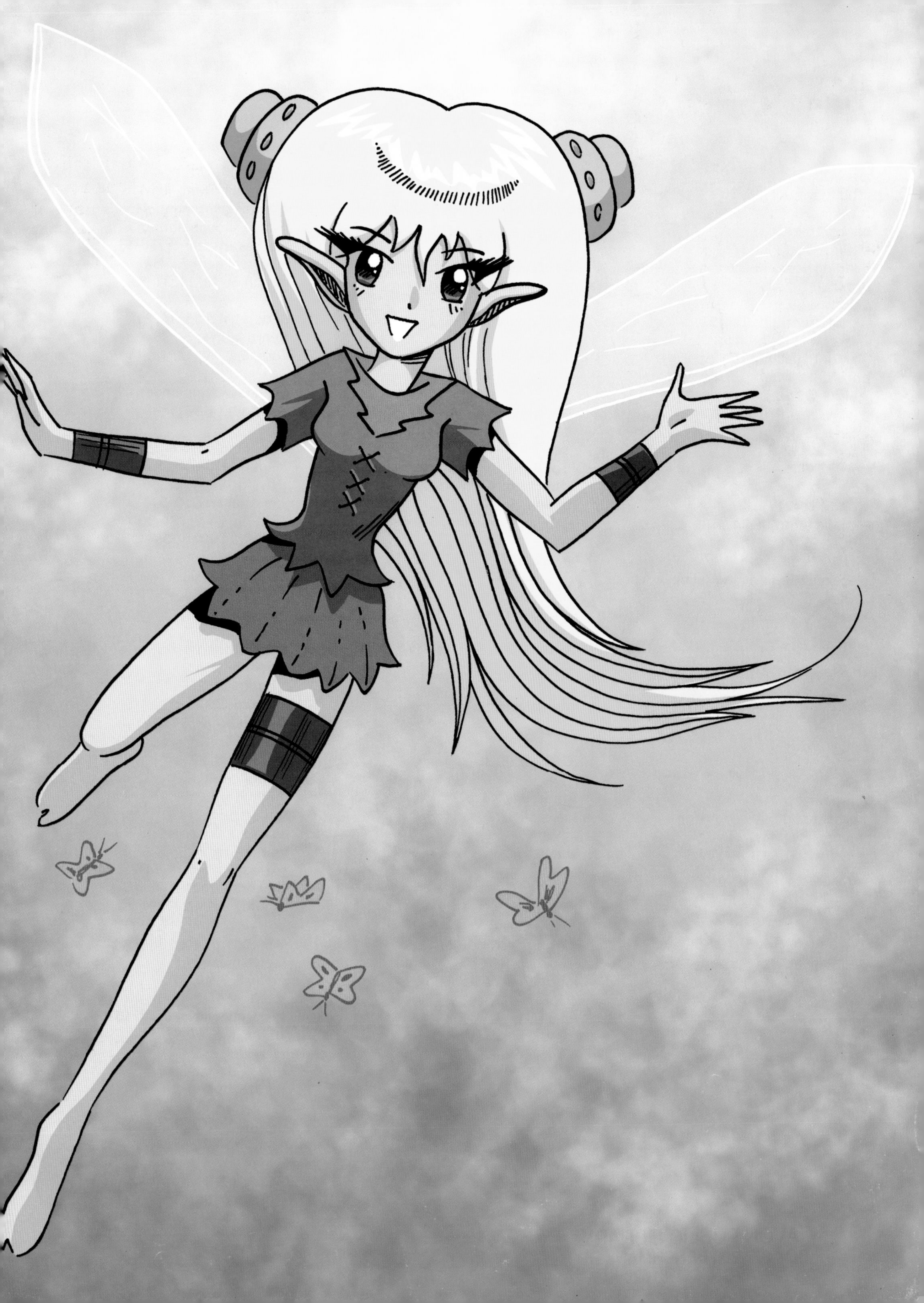

Index

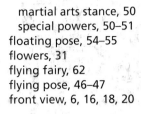